MW01124372

SMART
LEADERSHIP

How America's Top Leaders Boost Performance, Productivity
and Profitability by Creating Exceptional and Engaging Cultures

To my daughter, Abiygal

BRETT M. HUTTON

Brett 2015

emerge
publishing

TULSA, OKLAHOMA

17 16 15 14   10 9 8 7 6 5 4 3 2 1

SMART LEADERSHIP: *How America's Top Leaders Boost Performance, Productivity and Profitability by creating Exceptional and Engaging Cultures*

©2015 Brett M. Hutton

TULSA, OKLAHOMA

Published by:
Emerge Publishing, LLC
9521B Riverside Parkway, Suite 243
Tulsa, Oklahoma 74137
Phone: 888.407.4447
www.EmergePublishing.com

Cover Design: Christian Ophus | Emerge Publishing, LLC
Interior Design: Anita Stumbo

Library of Congress Cataloging-in-Publication Data
Hutton, Brett M.
Smart Leadership
ISBN: 13: 978-0-9907694-9-1
Printed in the United States of America.

Contents

Introduction

"Corporate culture can contribute meaningfully to financial results, and many people do not give this fact enough attention."
—John Kotter

One of the hottest comedy teams in the 1950s was Dean Martin and Jerry Lewis. Lewis was the comedian and Martin the straight man. When you watch clips of the two acting together, Lewis appears to be shorter than Martin. In a Larry King interview, Lewis revealed that he and Martin were actually the same height, but Lewis would work in a crouch for the comedic effect. Over the years while working in American business, I have often thought about this story because there have been times when I have had to work in a crouch (figuratively speaking) in order to make the politics work with those in management. I am confident I am not alone in this experience of corporate culture and believe that these "crouch cultures" have been far too prevalent in

American business, where those whom Jack Welch calls "the 70%" are expected to deliver an extraordinary performance while working from a crouch.

It is tragic that anyone would feel their company culture inhibits their ability to deliver exceptional results. Yet many leaders do not realize that they have themselves created the culture that is keeping their employees from delivering an exceptional performance. On the other hand, smart leaders are cognizant of how their decisions will impact their organizational culture. Smart leaders strive to create a culture where their employees can excel and reach their full potential.

Fortunately, there is a paradigm shift happening in American business that is impacting the way companies think about the importance of culture. While I was working on this project, books like *Conscious Capitalism* by John Mackey and Raj Sisodia and *Thrive* by Arianna Huffington hit the bookshelves. These works are indicative of the shift in traditional business mindsets. Companies like Google, Zappos and Starbucks have already made significant inroads in changing the old ways of doing business, all serving as significant examples of the changing paradigm of company culture. The up-and-coming millennial workforce is looking for companies that are choosing to take these newly paved roads.

Smart Leadership is a book about what it means to create an exceptional and engaging culture, a look at the different dynamics that shape company culture and how those dynamics impact employee performance, productivity and profitability. Whatever your company is on the outside, whether it is the product you produce, the service you deliver or the level of satisfaction your customers are experiencing, it is a reflection of what you are on the inside—your culture. Exceptional and engaging cultures boost performance and productivity and are the secret behind a profitable company.

Cultures are as unique as the people who work in them.

We should turn our attention to evaluating our culture in the same way we evaluate our people. All organizations have a culture; all cultures are created by values, good, bad or ugly. Whatever values are present in your organization's culture are there either by default or by design. Companies with cultures that are well designed and well defined in terms of core values tend to be much more successful. Successful companies intentionally and continuously build the right values into their culture.

Some would falsely assume you create a culture and then let it run on its own as if on autopilot, but culture is not static. Culture is a living, breathing entity. It is not easily cloned, it usually requires discovery and growth, and it is rarely instantly mature. Like any other living thing, it requires care and attention to grow and develop to maturity. We must have an "on purpose" culture.

Many successful companies that have been in existence for a while find that their cultures tend to become stubborn and unyielding to change. This is usually a product of hubris and this condition will many times go unchecked until some kind of crisis occurs. By his own admission, this is not unlike what happened to Starbucks when Howard Schultz made the decision to retake the position of CEO in 2008 as recounted in his book, *Onward.* In some instances, companies like Starbucks make the needed changes in a time of crisis and are able to pull up out of their nosedive before it is too late and survive. Some companies are not so fortunate and like the *Titanic,* they are unable to change course in time and so hit the proverbial iceberg and find themselves sunk, to their own shock and chagrin. It pays to slow down long enough to evaluate the current state of your company culture. Make no mistake: thriving companies are a product of thriving cultures.

The General Motors recall crisis hit the news early in 2014. If you look at the report that came out of their internal investigation, you notice right away that there were many different dynamics operating in their company culture. Some of those dynamics conflicted with one another, creating multiple disconnects. For example, it was a stated policy that safety was first priority, regardless of cost. But at the same time, bottom line numbers were watched very closely due to the threat of bankruptcy. This created duplicity in the culture, which often caused conflicting values. In addition, employees who raised safety concerns often received push-back from management because of the potential cost related to these concerns. These kinds of actions spoke much louder than any policy.

In the conclusion, the report did not identify any one spe-cific thing that could be blamed for the delay in resolving the defect except that the problem was somewhere in the GM culture. Whatever disconnects happened in the culture were most likely a result of multiple inconsistencies and conflict-ing values. Perhaps the greatest lesson we should all learn from the GM crisis is that failures in a company culture come at a very high cost. There is a currency to culture.

This is not a leader-bashing book. Leadership is not the villain here. The book's purpose is to show how poor or flawed leadership impacts culture. Smart leaders are open to self-examination and value the process of self-discovery as necessary to success. The purpose of this book is to help leaders identify the disconnects in their culture and find ways to eliminate them. Sometimes people know there is a problem, but just can't pinpoint the source or figure out how to verbalize what they are experiencing. The fact is cultures reflect a set of values, whether spoken or unspoken. The pre-vailing values of a company are based in the precedent set by the leadership. Whatever disconnects you have in your culture are a result of those prevailing values.

Leaders have the ability to unlock the talents and abilities in those they lead. By my definition, a leader is someone who unlocks the extraordinary potential in others. Many leaders can be naturally competitive, which is often the reason they were promoted to leadership in the first place. Unfortunately, an unbridled competitive nature can work against them in their effort to be effective leaders as they become combative when challenged by a dissenting opinion or threatened by an employee's ability more heightened than their own. Instead of unlocking the potential in others we end up blocking it. As leaders, we cannot effectively lead if we see the success of others as a challenge to our own success. We cannot be in competition with those who work for us. We must see ourselves as the cultivators of human potential.

Whether business, church, school, or other organization, people are attracted to culture. People naturally want to be in a place where they can grow, develop and invest themselves both personally and professionally. When growth and development are hindered, people recognize and feel the void. This book was birthed out of the leadership void I have experienced in my own life. Even though it is a compilation of ideas and concepts, it is my story, written in my voice.

There was some question about how to promote this book. Is it about leadership or about culture? It is a book about both. Company culture is driving your business and leadership is driving company culture. The two ideas are inseparable, and smart leaders recognize and understand the connection. ∎

CHAPTER ONE

Find The Laughter

Culture Is Driving Your Business

"Businesses often forget about the culture, and ultimately, they suffer for it because you can't deliver good service from unhappy employees."
—Tony Hsieh, CEO of Zappos

"Culture is the living, breathing heart of a business."
—Walter Robb, co-CEO of Whole Foods Market

I n the 2001 movie *Monsters, Inc.*, produced by Pixar, the story is centered on two monsters that work for an energy company called Monsters, Inc. The company generates electricity for a city by employing monsters to scare children in their bedrooms at night. The monsters access the children through closet doors that link from the company's scare floor directly to each child's room. The screams of the children are then bottled in canisters and used to provide the needed power for the monsters' city. Scaring is considered a very hazardous job because the monsters believe the children are toxic and any contact with them is deadly.

Soon after the story begins we are told the company is in trouble; production is down because children have become much more difficult to scare. To further complicate the situation, the recruiting of new hires isn't going well. We are given a peek into the scare training floor where we see new hires being trained to scare in a simulated child's room; failing miserably. It is more comical than scary and does not give the owner much reassurance for the future of his company.

The plot centers around two main characters: James P. Sullivan, a large and blue furry monster who goes by the nickname Sully and Mike Wazowski, a short, round, one-eyed creature. Sully and Mike are the number one scare team in the company, driven by the scream production capability of Sully. The conflict begins when Wazowski gets stopped by one of the supervisors because he has once again forgotten to file his paperwork for the evening. Wazowski has an important date that night, so Sully volunteers to take care of the paperwork so Wazowski can continue on and not upset his girlfriend. When Sully goes back to the scare floor, he discovers a door to some child's bedroom has been left active on the floor after hours. This arouses his suspicion so he investigates and discovers another scare monster named Randall, who appears to be cheating by entering a child's room after hours. He is Sully's main scare competitor and nemesis throughout the movie.

In the middle of this monster encounter, the little girl who lives in that room somehow finds her way into the factory through the active door. The rest of the story centers around Sully and Wazowski's efforts to sneak the child back into the human world without being caught. In the beginning, the monsters are terrified of the child, thinking she is toxic and a danger to them both. Randall, who is the child's regular scare monster, knows the child crossed from the human world to the scare floor and because of the risk that his cheating might be exposed, pursues Sully and Wazowski in an attempt to take the child.

The irony of the story is that the little girl is not at all afraid of the monster Sully. Sully begins to question the whole belief that children are toxic, as he has always been taught. In time, Sully becomes emotionally attached to the child and nicknames her "Boo." One of the things Sully and Wazowski discover in their interactions with Boo is that when the little girl laughs (usually at something Wazowski has said or done), it sends shock waves through the power grid. They find this very odd at first, not realizing the full implications of the phenomenon. The shock waves cause a problem as the more Boo laughs, the more difficult it is to keep her from being detected in the monster world. Initially, every effort is made to muffle the laughs. Later in the movie, however, Sully and Wazowski use the child's laughter to power the doors in the big warehouse chase, as they are running to escape Randall and restore Boo to the human world.

The story concludes with the owner of the company, Mr. Waternoose, being revealed as the mastermind behind Randall's cheating, struggling to salvage his failing company. Randall had developed a scream extractor and the master plan was that children would be kidnapped and hooked up to the machine to extract their screams by force. Once this evil plot is exposed by Sully and Mike, Boo is then restored to the human world, a saddening departure.

The great discovery in the movie is that children's laughter produces higher quantities of energy than their screaming. This discovery led to an entirely different approach to the way the power company did business. Now humor—not fear—was the driving force behind production. This resulted in a reversal of roles in the number one scare team, as Mike Wazowski, the comic, was now sent into children's bedrooms to make them laugh. To further emphasize the irony, the new hire monster at the beginning of the movie, whose performance was more comical than scary, now finds himself as one of the chief producers of energy by his ability to make children laugh.

The reason I indulged in such detail in recounting the storyline of this movie is because it illustrates in fiction what commonly happens in American business. For now, I will resist making the more obvious parallel that fear is far less productive than laughter and just point out instead that so many times, either because our current methods of production have worked in the past or may still currently be working but yielding fewer results, we stubbornly refuse to entertain any ideas outside of the business philosophy or methods we currently embrace. Things that made sense yesterday do not necessarily make sense today. As much as we like proven methods, it is usually the unproven methods that lead to new and innovative ideas. Of course, once the new idea is proven, everyone wants to jump aboard the train, secretly wishing they had been on board from the beginning.

Smarter Leaders Needed

We have smart phones, smart TVs and smart cars but where are the smart leaders? Whatever problems we have in our companies, we must acknowledge that they stem from problems in leadership. We need to be smarter leaders. The world needs smarter leaders. If you have been paying attention to leadership approval ratings, you know they are down worldwide. Those leaders enjoying success today have found new paradigms and new ways of thinking that shape their entire company culture beyond a mere slogan on the wall. Whether it is Tony Hsieh of Zappos "Delivering Happiness" or John

Mackey's "Conscious Capitalism" based Whole Foods or Howard Schultz's Starbucks, whose mission is to inspire and nurture the human spirit, in one sense or another, these leaders have found the "laughter" that has made their companies successful and profitable. One thing they have in common is that their paradigm focuses on bringing value to the whole of those who have a vested interest in the company, not just the shareholders. Even Jack Welch, a leadership giant and evangelist for an older paradigm, has said, "On the face of it, shareholder value is the dumbest idea in the world. Shareholder value is a result, not a strategy … your main constituencies are your employees, your customers and your products" (Guerrerra 2009). This is the mindset for the new emerging paradigm.

The mindset and attitude of leadership sets the entire tone of the culture. If you remember from *Monsters, Inc.*, the whole scare floor changed when the company moved away from scaring children to making children laugh. The floor was now filled with balloons, party decorations and celebration.

Your current culture says a lot about your business. Leadership either creates a culture where everything is kept under wraps, using fear as a driver, suppressing the people who work for them, or it allows people the freedom to develop and work independently out of what is inside of them. If you have experienced either of those scenarios, you know that one sucks the life out of you while the other supplies an energy that makes you want to get out of bed in the morning.

Those two scenarios are as different as day and night but leadership creates them both. We have a mindset that somehow the responsibility for exceptional performance solely rests with the employee. But smart leaders know that they have the power to create a culture that brings out the best in their employees and boost performance.

Finding Your Uniqueness

Imitation may be the highest form of flattery, but it is not always the guarantee of a successful business. I know one young entrepreneur who claims he builds his businesses by imitating others, but his own uniqueness still influences everything he does. Companies have their own unique personality, as unique as those who are employed within them. Look at the aforementioned Zappos, who built their company around a core strategy of "delivering happiness" to both the customer and their employees. They developed a whole business culture around this one idea. The uniqueness of that idea made the difference between Zappos being a good company and an exceptional one.

The goal of my book is to help put you on track to "find the laughter." For the purpose of this book, finding the laughter simply means discovering the underlying dynamics that influence and create an extraordinary and engaging culture. The underlying assumption being that an extraordinary culture facilitates extraordinary performance. Tony Hsieh said, "Our number one priority is company culture. Our whole belief is that if you get the culture right, most of the other stuff like delivering great customer service or building a long-term enduring brand will just happen naturally on its own."

Business is about discovering who you are and having a willingness to evaluate your progress along the way. When change is needed in your company, it will usually necessitate a change in culture. If you are looking for some technological scream machine that will improve production in your business, you have it all wrong. Technology is not enough to separate your company from everyone else. What will make your company stand out is the leadership's ability to create an engaging culture. But since culture affects innovation, the right culture can facilitate cutting edge ideas. Culture is the distinguishing mark of companies like Google, Whole Foods, Starbucks and others.

Wealth Is in Your People

Your gold mine is most likely right under your nose, inherent in the people who work for your company. You simply must create a culture that promotes them. By "promote," I don't mean in strictly the traditional sense of giving promotions (although that might help if promotions are overdue); I'm talking about promoting what is inside of them. You have undiscovered and untapped wealth in those who currently work in your company. You have star players you have not yet discovered because you have simply not provided a place for them to show off their skills. Extraordinary results are within your reach; you just need to adjust the way you think about a few things. Exceptional companies find the laughter, which they then weave into the fabric of their culture because they understand its currency. I invite you to discover the currency of culture. ▪

CHAPTER TWO

Vision
Making People Feel Like Insiders

"When you're surrounded by people who share a passionate commitment around a common purpose, anything is possible."
—Howard Schultz, CEO Starbucks

"Culture is not the most important thing in the world. It's the only thing. It is the thing that drives the business."
—Jim Sinegal, co-founder of Costco

According to *Merriam-Webster*, based on the top look ups at its online dictionary, culture was the most searched word out of 100 million lookups per month, making it the word of the year in 2014. Webster's Dictionary defines culture as "a way of thinking, behaving, or working that exists in a place or organization." According to Webster, culture can also have a biological application in that it can be "the act or process of cultivating living material." In keeping with the first definition, our way of thinking and

19

behaving impacts our way of working; it creates our culture. In keeping with the second definition, we must see our culture as something living, not static, and recognize that growth and development are part of the cultivating nature of an exceptional culture.

In the simplest terms, culture is a group of diverse people who have come together around a common goal. Culture is developed when a group of people come together who are like-minded in their approach to leadership, how they manage people and how they conduct their business. Culture is more than just environment; culture is shared beliefs, shared values and a shared purpose.

Culture is a way of thinking that impacts the way you view and treat your employees and your customers. The vision of some companies is heavily weighted toward considering the customer while failing to consider the employees. This is backwards. As with most things, what you are on the inside determines who you are on the outside. Howard Schultz of Starbucks and Tony Hsieh of Zappos both recognize that what employees are experiencing in their culture impacts how they treat their customers.

Vision
There are plenty of books that will tell you that you need a vision, books that tell you how to write a vision. But the essential dynamic is, how do you get people to buy into a vision, to follow the vision once it has been defined?

One of the base premises of this book is that leadership behaviors that build connection are good, while leadership behaviors that create disconnect are bad. Nothing positively affects the performance of an individual employee more than their sense of connection to the company and to its vision. In order to get people to buy into and follow the vision, they must feel connected to it. Simply writing words on paper, calling it a vision and posting it on the wall does not ensure connection.

Vision must touch something inside the individuals who make up the company. Higher retention levels are attained when that internal connection is made. In a healthy, thriving human body, all the parts are connected to both the head and the heart. In order to have a healthy, thriving company, the vision must make a connection with both the head and the heart.

Jonah Berger, in his book *Contagious,* tells us that in order for ideas to catch on, they must provide social currency. For Berger, this means that an idea must be communicated in such a way that it makes people feel like insiders. When vision makes those within the company feel like insiders, a connection is formed between employee and the company. This is the starting point for employee engagement.

For the purpose of this book, let's adapt that concept and instead of social currency let me introduce the idea of workplace currency. As we further define this idea, we will see that the level of workplace currency directly impacts the level of employee engagement. The higher level of currency produces a higher level of engagement. If we, as leaders, can develop and communicate the vision in a way that makes people feel like insiders, we elevate their sense of currency in the workplace—we make them feel connected and valuable. When people feel valuable, they are more engaged and invested in what they do. This translates into higher company retention levels.

Lee Cockerell, former senior operating executive of Walt Disney World, says leaders must create a place where everybody matters and they know they matter. People cannot create value in a place where they feel they have no value. It is contrary to human motivation. This is the starting point of a company vision: Making people feel like they matter and that they are a part of something that matters. Without this, there is no basis for connection.

Connection is a powerful thing. When we feel connected, we are motivated to invest ourselves. Daniel H. Pink contends in his book *Drive* that the secret to performance is to tap into people's intrinsic motivation, the desire for a sense of connection; to feel like an insider appeals to our intrinsic motivations. When we feel connected, we feel we have currency in our workplace.

Who Are We
Companies spend a lot of money and effort soliciting potential customers by answering the question "why us." But before we can answer that question, we must first ask "who us" and define who we are. Failure to answer this question means your company is at risk for multiple internal inconsistencies in its culture. Vision is the primary driver of culture. The culture of a company is set in place by the vision cast by its leaders. The vision is generally made up of three parts and establishes why we exist and answers the question who are we.

1. The purpose, which is one simple statement or idea that describes the impact your company will make on the larger global scale
2. The core strategy, usually expressed in a mission statement that should reflect the uniqueness of the company.
3. A set of core values, generally determined by company leaders, which support the core strategy.

People connect to purpose, global purpose. Don't underestimate the power of purpose for both your employees and your customers. For example, let's look in more detail at Howard Schultz's vision for Starbucks, taken from their website.

Mission Statement: To inspire and nurture the human spirit—one person, one cup and one neighborhood at a time.

The man sells coffee but has somehow, through elevating the vision of his company, created a brand that is iconic and known worldwide. If Howard Schultz can take coffee and give it global impact, you can create an idea that defines how your company is changing the world in some way. I love his summary statement that follows the core values: "We are performance driven, through the lens of humanity." Again, he elevates the motivation behind what they do.

The vision should be at the center of what you do as a company and it must translate into a definable, functioning culture. In other words, it must be living and breathing within the day-to-day process. In this way, vision becomes much more than words posted on the walls; it forms the heart and soul of a successful company.

When people have a clear, definitive vision to follow, they know what they are working and fighting for and that becomes the driving force behind their performance. That kind of vision motivates them from the inside out, inspiring them to reach higher. It certainly worked for Howard Schultz.

Let's hear what another iconic leader, Jack Welch, says about vision as it relates to the success of his system of differentiation:

"Differentiation starts with communication—exhaustive communication—of a company's mission (where it's going) and its values (the behaviors that are going to get it there). I'm not talking about putting a plaque on the lobby wall with the usual generic gobbledygook. I'm talking about a company's leaders being so specific, granular, and vivid about mission and values that employees could recite them in their sleep" (Welch 2013).

I appreciate the way in which Mr. Welch measures performance on the basis of how well an employee demonstrates the core values of the company, not just their numbers. I appreciate that he holds his leaders accountable for how well they communicate the vision, recognizing its importance to a successful culture.

Whether you have regard for your culture or not, it usually works something like this: Culture drives the business, leaders drive the culture, and the values of each individual leader drive them. Because you have the potential for so many value variations within the different leaders, you get a hodgepodge culture made up of those values—some good and some not so good. The preferred model is for leadership to develop a set of core values, this set of core values drives leadership behavioral values which in turn drives the culture. Leadership is still driving culture, but now within a parameter of established core values without variations. That way everything in the culture can be judged against these values.

I have seen leaders whose behavioral values run contrary to the vision and stated core values because who they are on the inside is contrary to both the vision and values. Likewise, you cannot hire leaders from the outside who values are not consistent with the company's vision and core values, regardless of their qualifications or track record. People will not connect to a vision if their leaders are not demonstrating the core values that support it in their actions in the day-to-day business of the workplace. This can create a huge disconnect between leaders and the people who work for them.

The core values of a company set the expectations for what people need to do to earn workplace currency. As mentioned earlier, workplace currency is simply defined as people having a sense of feeling valued and of being valuable within their company. This is why we care about promotions and titles even outside of money considerations, because the promotion or title gives us currency in the workplace. The higher the currency, the more control we feel we have over our job. This heightens our sense of security and lowers our feelings of uncertainty, raising our level of performance and productivity.

Ryan Carson, co-founder of Treehouse, an online education company, explains how at their company, they eliminated all levels of management. What Treehouse had found was that as they grew and added levels of management, there was an increase in rumors, politics and complaints (Carson 2013). The founders determined they had hired self-motivated people who were capable of self-management and the added levels of management were a hindrance, not a help, to productivity (Carson 2013). This bold move certainly leveled the playing field, as it created a more flat organizational structure within the culture by giving everyone in the company greater equality. The founders thought those who work at Treehouse should be considered adults and trusted to manage themselves.

Sometimes levels of management can diminish the currency of the non-management workforce. As I mentioned in the introduction, people feel like they have to work in a crouch in order to navigate the politics created by the hierarchy. At the extreme, this can be a very oppressive culture where people feel like they have to hold back and ultimately feel held back in their own growth and development. This was a very smart change by Treehouse in that it raised the level of currency across the company.

When people feel their workplace currency is diminished or limited, they often feel they need to fight for it if they are to have any hope of surviving in their job. Things quickly become political and adversarial and the essential culture dynamics of collaboration and communication suffer. This quickly becomes a life-sucking cancer within a hierarchical structure.

The core values of a company set the rules of the game. They say *this is the type of behavior that is rewarded.* What we are learning is that if core values are contrary to intrinsic motivators, they work against the establishment of an effective culture and eventually cause people to disconnect.

Examples of Iconic Vision

Whatever you think of Apple, there is no other company that so clearly demonstrates the impact of vision. From the beginning, the mission of Apple has been stated in two simple words: Think Different. They operated from the premise that it wasn't enough to look at the competition and say, "We are going to do it better"; the founders of Apple were committed to look at the competition and say, "We are going to do it differently." This idea drove the company from its inception, and then again when it came back under the leadership of Steve Jobs in 1997. As amazing and revolutionary as the iPod, iPhone and iPad have been, no single product that has come out of Apple has been as radical as the original idea of the personal computer, created from the belief that computers are for every person, not just big corporations. This idea alone, this way of thinking different, has changed the world. Let me add, this idea that computers are for everyone was not accepted by all and in fact was originally rejected by one time giants Xerox and IBM.

It would be natural to assume Apple is successful because of its products, but I would contend the vision was the chicken that produced the egg. Whether you like the products and gladly drink the Kool-Aid or not, you cannot deny the results. Bob Brochers, former Apple product manager, is reported to have told a group of students that Apple's idea for the iPhone was initially rooted in a small handful of tightly focused concepts centered around breaking the rules of the game while paying attention to detail and helping people "think differently" about the way they associate with their smartphones (Wray 2012). Looking back at the history of the iPhone, we can easily see how this vision, which was fully embraced by employees, translated into a global customer impact. Vision can and should impact culture in order to be meaningful, creating a connection for both employee and customer.

Another company with a simplistic vision statement is Zappos. Unlike Apple, Zappos didn't have a well-defined core strategy in the beginning. Tony Hsieh of Zappos waited six years before he wrote out the company's mission statement that became their core strategy: To provide the best customer service possible. But there was another idea underlining their culture: Delivering Happiness. For Tony, delivering happiness went beyond only making the customer happy; it meant making sure employees were happy as well. Tony felt that happy employees would be more likely to make happy customers. This deliberate decision to focus on the experience of employees naturally connected the employees to the vision and therefore, the vision had both internal and external influence.

By the time Hsieh birthed the mission statement, the Zappos culture was already in place and growing. He simply defined on paper what was already there and functioning within the day-to-day business. In this way, the Zappos culture was very organic, developing over time out of what already existed within the leaders and employees that made up the company. It is much easier for a start-up to cultivate their culture organically. But even within an established company that has an antiquated culture, smart leaders should consider the internal makeup of the people who work there when instituting a change. Just ask Ron Johnson, who was responsible for the success of Apple's retail stores and was later hired by JC Penney. He unsuccessfully attempted to take the same cultural paradigm from the Apple retail stores and change the culture of JC Penney. He learned that JC Penney is not Apple. Every company has an organic nature to it; it is what gives a company its authenticity.

Apple and Zappos differed slightly in their approach to defining their culture. One said, "This is who we are going to be." The other said, "This is who we are." An authentic vision is a convergence of the two. Let me explain. Since you build a company with people, if you say this is who we are going to be, you must find people who define themselves in a way that aligns with that idea. The "who we are" of the people must match the "this is who we are going to be" of the vision. Otherwise there is negative polarization in your culture.

Both Apple and Zappos experienced success even though their approaches were somewhat different. If, like Zappos, you choose to allow your mission statement to develop out of who you are, allow yourself a time of discovery. Tony Hsieh took six years to develop the Zappos mission statement. He resisted writing a mission statement because it reminded him of the corporate culture he had rejected, and no doubt that time of discovery probably cost him some money, but you can't argue with the end result. If your focus is to only make money in the short term, allowing your vision to develop organically is going to be a challenge for you. But part of branding is determining who we are.

The Value of Authenticity

For a culture to be both extraordinary and engaging there has to be authenticity in its creation. If a culture develops organically, there can be no doubt about its authenticity. As I said earlier, it is easier for a start-up culture to develop organically, because there is nothing in the culture to undo or redefine, but every company has its own inbred authenticity. When a company's authenticity is discovered and defined, it develops an immediate connection between the people and the vision. There is less need to "force" employees to conform to a vision written on the wall, because the vision is already making an internal connection. In a sense, it is already written on their hearts because there is a connection of common purpose. Remember, culture is the bringing together of people around a common purpose supported by defined core values; this is the baseline connection. With the internal connection the likelihood of employee disconnect is greatly diminished. When Ron Johnson was hired by JC Penney to turn the faltering company around, he attempted to introduce a new vision to the existing culture and it created disconnect with the employees instead of connection. He didn't consider the organic nature of the JC Penney culture. This would prove to be his undoing. He was ousted after 17 months (Tuttle 2013).

Most companies either ignore or don't understand the organic nature of culture. They think the vision on the wall is driving their business, or at least they hope it is. The value in your business is derived from the diversity and uniqueness of the people who make up the company; they are what drive it. Look at the common core values that are already being exhibited by the people who make up your business. Let the synergy of those common core values define who you are as a company. People with common core values tend to naturally connect with each other even when the values are not well defined.

A common mistake is to see the company first, focusing on it as the primary entity (in some cases the deity) at which everyone works and serves. Without people, a company is just a name, brick and mortar. The living, breathing part of the company is the people. For this reason, vision is not just about defining a company; it is about defining the people who work there *and it is being defined by the people who work there, all in one motion.* There is something about an organic vision that has an element of life in it. Call it humanity or something else; whatever you want to call it, people connect to it. It creates an authenticity that can potentially set you apart from everyone else in your industry.

If you are saying we want to be just like Apple or just like Zappos, you are missing the point. Their successes are a result of discovering the uniqueness and authenticity within themselves.

Teach Them to Think Like Owners

My wife and I have owned houses but in other seasons of our life, we have been renters. Nevertheless, whether we own or rent, we always think like owners. This ownership mindset drives us to take better care of the houses we rent. On the other side, our landlords differed in the way they treated us. With one of the houses we rented, we had a wonderful landlord who treated us like we were owners. In contrast with another house we rented where the landlord treated us like renters. While our personal commitment to think like owners drove us to maintain a certain level of care for both houses, we noticed that our level of care for the first house was greater than the level of care we exhibited for the second. The way we were treated by our landlords impacted the level of care and attention we gave to the houses in which we lived. We disliked the way we were treated (like renters) by the second landlord and so as soon as our lease was up, we moved. Even with as much trouble and expense as moving involves, my wife refused to give that second landlord one more cent past our contracted lease. In short, what made the difference was whether or not the landlord treated us with dignity and respect.

If your employees are acting like renters in their job, it is probably because you are treating them like renters. Are you following my analogy? So many of these employees have never known what it is like to be treated like owners and therefore, they don't know how to think like owners. If you will instill in your people a sense of ownership and teach them to think like owners, you will see their level of performance rise. We've all heard the phrase "own it." When people have a sense of ownership, it raises their level of responsibility and creates higher levels of currency, as they feel more invested. Smart leaders promote a culture in which people at every level feel a sense of ownership and a greater investment in the success of the company. People connect to the vision when they feel they "own it." Employees are no longer simply task oriented; they are purpose driven. If they own it, you can be assured they are connected to it.

Do you want your workers to show up early and work late? Do you want to see higher levels of motivation in your people? Give them a sense of ownership. People are wired to desire ownership and when they are denied it, they feel less invested than they should be and their productivity suffers. Simply chaining people to a task limits the potential of what they could deliver, even if they are performing at acceptable levels. You must provide opportunities for your people to function outside of the task they have been given. One of the biggest ways to accomplish this is to make them part of the thought behind the process, not just part of the process. Then they will understand the why behind the task. If all of a sudden you show that you care and value what they think, once the shock wears off, it will so energize them that they will act like Snoopy at supper time.

A culture will cause people to flourish or flounder. People who already think like owners oftentimes will overcome a bad culture for a season, but eventually they will go find a culture where they have a sense of ownership. Why not create something that facilitates growth and development instead of hindering it? Why not create an exceptional and engaging culture?

The Value of Diversity

Many leaders will create a culture based on forced com-
pliance and conformity to the vision. They do it at the expense of diversity. Diversity should be embraced. To impose
a forced conformity is easier but you cheat yourself out of
building a highly innovative and creative culture. The secret
in managing that diverse group of people is pulling them together toward a single common purpose. The advantage of
defining core values is that it helps harness diversity, uniting
your people in pursuit of a common goal. Core values eliminate rogue management styles. Holding to clearly expressed
core values will not suppress diversity, but will rather provide
a value framework in which people of diverse backgrounds
and skill sets can flourish.

I have been a part of cultures in which everything was
dictated by the person at the top and everyone was forced to
conform to the thinking or vision of that one person. These
types of cultures are characteristically ruled by fear and control. Any departure from what is dictated is met with swift
retribution, as you are branded as a non-conformist and a
divergent. You are treated as an outsider and are at risk of
joining the unemployed. Organizations take this stance to
their own peril. Remember, Rudolph the Red-Nosed Rein-
deer was branded as a non-conformist and treated as an outsider, but he turned out to be the hero and later saved the
family business. Cultures that are dictated by fear and control
from the top, which refuse to accept diverse ideas, may seem
to be on the fast track to unity, as things appear to run more
smoothly. But do not be deceived: Forced unity is not true
unity. Forced unity is typically characterized by oppression
and limited thought and is, therefore, less productive.

Smart leaders recognize that you can only foster true unity when you embrace the diversity that is within the people who work for you. In simple terms, embracing diversity

means you recognize that everyone has something unique to bring to the table. Unity is achieved when you effectively manage that diversity into a single force to accomplish the common mission. Conformity, on the other hand, suppresses the unique differences in each person and therefore quenches creativity and innovation. It is evidence that management just doesn't think much of their people beyond their ability to complete the task they have been assigned.

Open-Minded Leaders
The success or failure of a company culture is often determined by whether or not the thought processes of the leaders remain fluid and open. A leader's thought process must remain receptive to new ideas, even if those new ideas challenge his initial thoughts. This keeps the culture from becoming static or stubborn. Open-mindedness is a desirable and necessary characteristic of effective leadership. Herb Kelleher, former CEO of Southwest Airlines, says, "You can't really be disciplined in what you do unless you are humble and open-minded. Humility breeds open-mindedness—and really, what we try to do is establish a clear and simple set of values that we understand. That simplifies things; that expedites things."

In summary, define the difference your company wants to make on the global scale and make it something to which people can connect. Write the vision and display it so your people can see it. Verbally communicate it as often as you have opportunity. Most of all live it in front of them. ∎

CHAPTER THREE

Disconnect

What Conflict Is Telling You

"A business as a machine does not, and cannot, have any social consciousness or social responsibility. A business viewed as a living entity is, like all people within a society, a citizen with a social and moral responsibility to both itself and society. A machine does not learn and adapt to its environment, but adaptation is the very essence of all living entities. Machines merely produce, they cannot innovate, while living entities can actually dream of and create a healthier future."

—John Mackey, co-CEO of Whole Foods Market

D isconnect is the enemy in your culture. General Motors failed to effectively resolve a car safety issue—a defective ignition switch—for eleven years because of disconnects in their organizational structure. Their own internal investigations into this matter resulted in a report recommending a re-examination of their culture (Valukas

2014). At the time of this writing, the defect has account-ed for 19 deaths (Isidore 2014) and the recall of around 29 million vehicles. The cost to the company's earnings is es-timated at $1.2 billion—in just one quarter alone (Bennett 2014). Three hundred fifteen pages of the GM internal inves-tigation report were dedicated to identifying disconnects in the GM culture, and as I stated in the introduction (in case you skipped it), the report was unable to attribute the failure to resolve the safety issue to any one specific disconnect. In my assessment, the culture had so many potential internal conflicts and contradictions that management had become incapable of effectively addressing them all and so they went unresolved, resulting in a devastating cost to the company and the public. They had become bound by the very culture they had created.

Nothing is more detrimental than disconnect in business. Disconnect is the reason your people are not reaching higher levels of performance and productivity. Think of the electric-ity flowing through your house. If the lights won't come on in one of the rooms, you know that somewhere there is a dis-connect that is keeping the electricity from that room. May-be a breaker is blown or maybe the switch is bad. Whatever it is, disconnect is your problem. The primary job of leadership is to identify disconnects and eliminate them, even if they are the ones creating them.

Your organizational structure may be designed like a tree, but it functions like a body. There is nothing more complex but yet perfectly connected, organized and unified as the hu-man body. I am surprised businesses haven't used the human body as an organizational model. Every part is connected by a joint and dependent on the other. As we emphasized in the second chapter, smart cultures put a great deal of focus on connection, first connecting people to the vision and then connecting people to each other. Just as eliminating disconnect is the job of leadership, so is promoting and maintaining connection within the culture.

The most notable characteristic of the human body is that every part communicates with the brain, regardless of how far away it is. Every part of the body receives direct impulses from the brain, creating a unified movement. As I mentioned in the first chapter, every part of the body is equally connected to and dependent on the heart as well as the head. In all my years in corporate America, I am still amazed at the amount of distance that often exists between managers and employees and how that distance impedes effective communication, creating one of the more common disconnects in American business. One of the most glaring things in the GM internal report was how disconnected the top leaders were to what was happening in regards to the safety issue. Representative Diana DeGette had this to say to GM's CEO Mary Barra:

> *"The report singles out many individuals at GM who made poor decisions or failed to act, but it doesn't identify one individual in a position of high leadership who was responsible for these systemic failures. The report absolves previous CEOs, the legal department, Ms. Barra and the GM Board from knowing about the tragedy beforehand. But that is nothing to be proud of"* (Hirsch and Puzzanghera 2014).

In all fairness, I have had managers who made it a point to interact with their employees. I have also had managers who did not. Even those managers who have no direct reports are still viewed as representing upper management, and people notice if you are stand-offish. You would be surprised how much trust you can build by just showing your face once in a while, genuinely making an effort to bridge the distance and connect with employees. But in your efforts to communicate, don't play favorites and spend all your time visiting with just one or two select few. Doing so will have the opposite effect on those who perceive they are not the favorites. As a manager, I make the extra effort to connect with the ones I initially struggle to communicate with, in order to eliminate the possibility of future disconnects.

Continuing with the body analogy, when a part of your body separates from the joint, we say it is disjointed. In the same way, when any part of your organization is disconnected, it is disjointed. The effectiveness of that disjointed part is compromised, as it no longer functions at full capacity. The tendency is to focus on the lack of performance of the disjointed part when the real problem is that the part is simply disconnected from the whole. I have seen this happen to individuals as well as whole departments.

If teams are pitted against each other, you have set your business up for disconnect. Above the performance of an individual team is the need for every team to be productive as part of the larger framework of teams. Only when you have healthy joints connecting each team to the other will all teams be able to function optimally to benefit the whole. The connection is what raises the performance level of each individual and the performance level of all the teams. I don't believe extraordinary performance can be achieved without this kind of connection. This is where ego and hierarchy must bow to the greater good of the organization. Didn't you see *Star Trek II: The Wrath of Khan*? Here is the dialogue from the scene where Spock is dying from saving the ship.

Kirk: *Spock!*
Spock: *The ship ... out of danger?*
Kirk: *Yes.*
Spock: *Don't grieve, Admiral. It is logical. The needs of the many outweigh ...*

Kirk: *... the needs of the few ...*
Spock: *... Or the one.*
(Personally, I cried at this scene.)

Despite the socialistic overtones here, this kind of mindset should be an inherent part of the core values of the culture and will serve as a safeguard against those who are there only to serve their own self-interest. Those who only serve their own interest disregard the impact their actions can have on the vested interest of others.

One of my first jobs was with a bank in Texas. I was told the former CEO would pit his departments against each other. For example, he would tell his mortgage group he wanted to increase the sale of mortgages by a certain percentage and then tell his underwriters to tighten up their underwriting standards. The result being that the underwriters were approving fewer mortgages, while at the same time the mortgage bankers were trying to raise their percentage of closings. As you might guess, this promoted a great deal of unnecessary stress and frustration.

A more recent setting in which I was involved, a manager made a habit of giving the same assignment to two different groups. When asked about the logic behind this idea, the manager replied, "I do it to see which group finishes the assignment quicker." I'm sure he thought this was smart leadership. I think it was a set-up for disconnect, failure, and frustration on the part of those who would later find out that their efforts had been duplicated. What about the wasted resources? Now let's be honest, what he was doing, well that was just stupid.

When people experience enough disconnects and the frustration that comes with them, they begin to disengage from their jobs. They may keep their head in the game in order to keep their job, but their heart is disengaged. You cannot have an exceptional culture where extraordinary performance is achieved unless both the heads and hearts of your employees are engaged.

People generally will not continue to work in a culture that brings them frustration. In order to alleviate the problem (outside of just leaving the company), they simply lower their expectations to avoid further disappointment. Unfortunately, by lowering their expectations, they have taken the first step toward disconnect in their job. Strong performers can usually continue to perform at a level that will allow them to keep their job, but any employee in this state of mind is no longer delivering an exceptional performance. When performance drops, we should not restrict our evaluation to the employee only but give some attention to the possibility that failures on the part of leadership can contribute to the drop in performance.

Allow me to go back to the body analogy again. In an organization, leaders function like the joints of the body. They connect their team to other teams based on where they fit into the organization. When disconnect occurs at the leadership level, everything breaks down. Team Hand is connected to Team Forearm by the wrist and Team Forearm is connected to Team Bicep by the elbow, and so on and so on. Whatever the team needs is supplied through the joint. In a very real sense, leaders control the flow of information to the employees.

I have seen leaders withhold information because in keeping it to themselves, they thought it kept them in power. What they failed to realize was that by withholding the flow of information, they made it more difficult for their people to do their job, diminishing their performance and lowering their productivity. Smart leaders supply whatever is needed to boost performance, seeing it as their responsibility to enable other people to do their jobs.

Leaders who communicate well with other departments and with their own people give their team and their company a great advantage. Because their team is connected to the whole, it facilitates a unified sharing and free flow of the knowledge and tools needed for the team to perform. This positions their people for high levels of productivity, making it a win for everyone. The kind of power play where someone, especially a leader, is hoarding knowledge creates a very dysfunctional culture and a very obvious disconnect.

Let's say your brain is only communicating to certain parts of your body. You want to move forward, but your ankle is not getting the information. This means your foot can't perform and your toes can't do their job. Your leg and knee are trying to compensate because the ankle is not performing, so they are working harder. Are you getting the picture? You would look, shall we say, challenged! All because one part of your body is not getting the information needed to perform its job to move your body forward.

The great thing about the makeup of your body is that the part farthest away from the brain—your toes—still gets the same quality signals from the brain that every other part gets. This enables your body to function and move in one unified direction toward its desired goal. Our body is the perfect model for unity and singleness of purpose. It is a great model for any organizational structure.

The Value of Every Part

You cannot afford to treat any member of your organization as lesser than another. To keep with the body metaphor, that would be like saying I don't really need my toes. My knees don't really matter. My guess is that there is not a single part of your body you want to do without. Make sure all the parts of your business are functioning in their full capacity by giving them the needed tools and value they deserve. Smart leaders understand the value of every single member of their business and that every part must be connected properly to each other. If I am a part of your business and I am not being or feeling valued, I am already in disconnect. Value is the first order of connection and connection is the basis of unity. Unity is an absolute necessity if you want to realize extraordinary results in business.

Under-Managed

According to a study by Rainmaker Thinking, Inc., the greatest disconnect of the workplace is under-management, with nine out of ten leaders/managers/supervisors consistently failing to provide the basics of management to their immediate staff (Tulgan 2014). With those statistics, it's no wonder Rainmaker called this an epidemic.

Rainmaker found that the overwhelming common denominator in cultures where extraordinary performance was not being realized is the lack of proper management. Please don't misunderstand what I'm saying. This is not a call for micromanagement, but one for proper management basics. These basics include things like managers communicating a clear picture of what is being asked of an employee in terms of their assigned task and providing the tools and resources to accomplish the assignment.

One of the immediate consequences of under-managing identified by Rainmaker is that these types of managers are held in lower regard by their direct employees. Since these under-managers do not implement purposeful strategies for managing their people, the desired growth and development of their employees is non-existent. Under-managers do not properly identify performance levels, so there is no way for employees to judge where they are in their development and therefore, they are unsure of their future path with the company.

42

My own experience has shown that if performance levels are not adequately identified, the result is low level performers are ignored, mediocre performers are many times advanced (for the wrong reasons), and high level performers go unrecognized and become frustrated from being overlooked. Under-management creates a vacuum where people cannot grow or develop and, when prolonged, it contributes to employee disengagement.

The Rainmaker report states that under-managers don't know they are under managing. In fact, five out of ten think they are doing a good job. This is a serious disconnect. Guess who suffers at review time? The employee, of course. But try convincing a manager that the performance levels of their employees are directly related to their ability to manage. Let me know how that conversation works out for you. In my experience, managers tend to look out for each other so it is difficult, if not impossible, to get your manager's manager to correct the problem. This leaves the employee feeling they have no advocate, creating other trust-related issues and leading to inevitable disconnect because they feel no one has their back.

Rainmaker offers a few reasons, based on their research, why managers often under-manage. Managers often find themselves in "firefighting mode." They move from one urgent problem to another. Problems that could have been avoided with better planning and solved easier if addressed before they became urgent. They simply went unidentified or ignored.

Another reason Rainmaker gives for under-managing is when firefighting mode has subsided, the manager's focus is on catching up and so they let their management of direct reports go on "autopilot." My observation has been that when firefighting mode is over, everyone is catching their breath and little time is given to addressing smaller problems that will later lead to the next four-alarm fire. Rainmaker says that moving from firefighter to autopilot becomes a vicious cycle that prohibits managers from being effective in performing basic management practices.

Perception and Disconnect

Conflict is the red flag that some kind of disconnect has occurred. When my son was in second grade, his teacher would take the class on field trips. A student leader from the class was appointed by the teacher to lead each field trip. On one particular trip, the class walked to the downtown area where we lived and my son was the appointed leader. This put my son at the front of the group and his teacher was at the very back.

When they came up to a corner where they needed to cross the street, for some reason, a group of kids at the front just took off running. This started the whole class running.

My son in his young second grade mind thought to himself, "I am the appointed leader. I need to get in front of these people," and so he took off running. From the teacher's view at the back of the line, all she could see was her class dangerously running across a main street of downtown. Of course, her immediate thought was that my son had led her class in the run across the street.

I received a call from the principal informing me that my son had led his class in a run across a downtown street. The teacher, being very upset, had immediately banned him from future field trips as his punishment.

When my son returned home that day, I asked him what happened and he explained his version of the story, just as I have told it you. My next question to my son was, "Did you tell the teacher what you just told me?" He said no, she wouldn't let him explain. Now I am sure your immediate response to this story is to cry out for vindication for my son because of how unfair and how unjust the teacher was to him (that was my immediate response), but I can tell you that I see this same kind of thing in business all the time.

Let's look at the basic elements of this story. First, the teacher's conclusion was based on her perception from her view at the back of the line. That perception had no basis in what really happened but it formed the basis for her conclusions and dictated the punishment she assigned my son. Second, there was no effort or apparent interest to try to find out what really happened. My son's teacher neither asked him any questions nor gave him the opportunity to give his version of what happened. More than likely, even if he had been able to give his version, it would have been discounted or discredited. The irony of the story is that he was trying to do the right thing and live up to the expectation that had been placed on him to properly lead the group.

The teacher's perception-based conclusion became the reality that my son now had to live in. It was her version that was reported to his principal and parents. His punishment was based on her conclusions, even though they were not accurate. Is this picture starting to take shape in your mind? Starting to hit close to home? If not, let me see if I can fill in the blanks. What happened to my son happens frequently in business. Someone's perceptions, usually a leader's, become the reality in which others much operate. Such are the common building blocks of conflict.

A smart leader cannot lead out of perception. He must find out what actually is true. Like my son's teacher, I am amazed how many leaders don't even ask questions before they jump to a conclusion. In some cases if they are getting the story from someone else, they simply make assessments based solely on the one side of the story. To resolve conflict properly, you must ask questions in order to move beyond surface appearances. You must determine where the true disconnect is in order to effectively resolve the right problem. If you haven't assessed the right problem, you have not resolved the right conflict.

My millennial children will tell you that whenever two or more of them had a conflict, I would never make a judgment before giving each person an opportunity to tell their side of the story. I can tell you that rarely did I find that the fault ever fell 100% all on one child. Now that my kids are grown, they too will get all sides of a story before making a judgment and rarely jump to any conclusions solely based on appearance. If my son's teacher had only asked the simple question, "What happened?" and given him the opportunity to provide an explanation for his actions, the final outcome could have been totally different.

Never underestimate the effect bias has on our initial judgment. Because of bias, we tend to believe what we want to believe, regardless of what the truth may be. That is why bias is often the perpetrator of disconnect. I worked for one particular man who, once his opinion of you began to shift to the negative, became very elaborate in the things he would make up in his mind about you. It would get to the point in a time of conflict that any attempt at a rational conversation was useless. He had constructed such a vivid image in his head, he was absolutely convinced he was right and what he thought was indeed the truth. Unfortunately, he was often so far from the truth that no conflict resolution was even possible. But that was okay with him, as his goal was not resolution but separation. Sadly, his arguments and conclusions justified the separation even though they were erroneous.

Leadership of this type lacks integrity. Everyone can see that this kind of leader is operating out of his own bias and therefore, any basis of trust within the culture is greatly diminished or completely destroyed. No one in the organization speaks up, however, because by doing so, they would put themselves at risk of receiving the same kind of unscrupulous scrutiny. In many instances, this type of leader is allowed to continue without challenge so real problems are unidentified and conflicts go unresolved.

Smart leaders understand that effective conflict resolution is based on what's right, rather than just on who's right. If all parties involved know that you are attempting to assess what is true without bias or prejudice, then you establish trust, and real conflict resolution requires trust. People will submit to the decisions of their leaders who demonstrate they can be trusted by listening to all sides of the story and not prematurely jumping to perception-based conclusions. Think about the alternative. When you think you have resolved a conflict but the resolution is based in erroneous assessments, the real problem is now buried deeper under the rubble of false conclusions until the day it resurrects itself and demands proper resolution. If you think this sounds a little dramatic (I was going for poetic), read the 2014 General Motors story for yourself and make your own assessment.

Here is a quote from Jody Gittell, author of *The Southwest Airlines Way,* a book about a company that has a track record for successfully handling conflict:

"Organizations should proactively seek out conflicts rather than allowing them to fester. Then managers should bring the parties together to better understand each other's perspective. If organizations do not identify and resolve cross-functional conflicts, those conflicts will weaken critical relationships of shared goals, shared knowledge, and mutual respect. When managers treat cross-functional conflict as an occasion for learning, they strengthen relationships between employees and boost performance of the work processes in which those employees are engaged" (Gittell 2003).

What Conflict Is Telling You

What conflict is telling you is where your disconnects exist. Healthy conflict can and will be the impetus for future growth if the disconnects are assessed and resolved properly. Conflict resolution can improve and enhance connection. Even when there is a dissenting thought or opinion, it can be the synergy for creative thought. Many leaders attempt to minimize conflict by suppressing all dissenting thoughts, behaviors and opinions. Any type of feedback is discouraged and receives pushback. Yet the organization eventually suffers from this type of leadership. It is all contingent on how leadership views diversity. Diversity can be the greatest asset of your culture. You can have the benefits of diversity and protect your culture from dissension by implementing this one idea. We call it collaboration. ∎

CHAPTER FOUR

Collaboration
The Foundation of a Great Culture

"In the United States, there is a myth of the lone genius coming up with brilliant ideas that change the world. While that occasionally happens, the more common scenario is that an individual comes up with an idea and shares it with other members of his or her team; they become excited and improve upon it. The spirit of collaboration allows the idea to evolve and mature."
—John Mackey, co-CEO Whole Foods Market

"Remember: You'll be left with an empty feeling if you hit the finish line alone. When you run a race as a team, though, you'll discover that much of the reward comes from hitting the tape together. You want to be surrounded not just by cheering onlookers but by a crowd of winners, celebrating as one."
—Howard Schultz, CEO Starbucks

An exceptional and engaging culture must have as its primary core value, collaboration. Webster's defines collaboration as "working jointly with others or together in an intellectual endeavor." Notice Webster's use of the words "working jointly," in light of my analogous use of the body as an organizational model with the emphasis on connecting joints. There is a supply and sharing of resources when we are connected. Everything is about connecting the individual parts to the whole. This is why collaboration is the indispensable value of company culture, because it creates and demands connection.

Indulge me a moment as I entertain a different metaphor. Think of collaboration as the concrete of your company's organization. Just as a house uses concrete for the foundation, collaboration is the stabilizing foundation to your company's culture. Most people think competition is the key to a successful business, but if competition isn't built upon a framework of collaboration, you will have problems. Nations collapse from within; so do companies.

There are three fundamental dynamics of collaboration: communication, information and inclusion. Communication is first because of its essential relationship to collaboration in a successful business management system. Let me illustrate. If you know anything about construction, you know that concrete is poured around steel rebar to make the concrete more structurally sound and to ensure that it will stay together. Without the steel, the concrete could not successful hold all the weight placed on it and it would collapse. In the same way, communication is the steel that reinforces and gives structural solidity to collaboration. If you've ever seen rebar before the concrete is poured, you know that it is configured as a structural grid within the foundation and is interconnected with steel ties. What a perfect picture of how collaboration and communication should work together. Communication within your company is that interlocking grid that provides your business with a structurally sound foundation on which you can build a successful culture. The biggest disconnects I see in business occur when collaboration and communication are absent or poorly executed in the organization. They are foundational to an exceptional and engaging culture.

Communication

There has been an expansion of technology aimed at improving communication. The advancement of instant messaging services and email, just to name a few technologies, should mean that we are now masters of communication. Though useful, the reality is these can easily become substitutes for real conversation—real communication. I have heard leaders complain when they were copied on some huge spreadsheet from another department, saying they couldn't make sense of what they received. This is primarily because they didn't have a context for the information contained in the spreadsheet. That context could be found in the actual conversations, the thought processes that surrounded the assimilation of the information. Ironically, I have often seen those same leaders turn around and do the same thing to another group of people, expecting them to understand the emailed material without including them in the actual conversation. Being invited into the middle or the end of a conversation puts people at a distinct disadvantage compared to those who were there from the beginning. If it is a conversation that impacts their job, it can have a negative impact on their ability to perform.

A summary email is no substitute for a face-to-face conversation in terms of effective communication. Don't get me wrong; I was born for email. Oftentimes it gives me the opportunity to assimilate my thoughts without being interrupted. In some instances, I have had to work very hard just to get "cc'd" on an email so I could stay in the loop, but a "cc" is not the end all. People need to be invited to and involved in the conversation as much as is practicably possible.

The hierarchal organization tree can be the greatest

inhibitor of both collaboration and communication. Going back to the picture of the human body as an example of good organizational structure, my toes are the furthest part of my body away from my head, but my brain communicates as effectively with them as with other parts in closer proximity. Why? Because my toes need the same quality of communication to perform their assigned task. I don't go anywhere without my toes. I cannot afford to have some kind of communication disconnect with my toes and still expect to be able to walk or run proficiently. I could cut off my old toes and have new ones attached, but good communication is still required for the new toes to function properly. The same is true in your business. Communication is the primary means you have to keep all the parts of your company functioning in unity. When communication is lacking, everyone's performance suffers.

Let us consider a company that lives or dies based on their collaborative effort and their ability to effectively communicate. Southwest Airlines has a workforce of approximately 45,000 people with diverse skill sets and different levels of experience. The employees are both union and non-union workers (according to statistics found on the Southwest Corporate Fact Sheet, the airline is approximately 83% unionized). Considering its size and the nature of their business, this looks like a recipe for huge disconnects (no pun here), and yet Southwest is a company known for its unified company culture and collaboration between the various groups, which they call "tribes." How has disconnect been averted in all these years since the company's inception in 1971?

In her book *The Southwest Airlines Way,* Jody Gittell details the practices Southwest has implemented across the company to promote collaboration and foster effective communication to cultivate a culture where employees can perform at extraordinary levels. They have created a culture where a great deal of attention is placed on a set of shared core values (safety, on-time performance and creating satisfied customers), which means that everyone is moving in the same direction toward a common purpose. Frontline employees have the opportunity to join in the problem-solving process at any level. In addition, the frontline supervisors work alongside their people doing the same job, acting as "player coaches" and a resource for resolving problems.

Southwest uses conflict resolution as a means to strengthen communication. Parties in dispute are proactively encouraged to work through their differences. Management steps in when necessary, not to discipline, but to act as mediators who guide the parties to a resolution. This process results in the development of a high level of trust and respect between employees and managers.

Even outside relationships that are traditionally considered volatile are handled differently at Southwest. The company views labor unions as partners rather than adversaries and communications between the company and labor leaders reflect that view. Southwest is up front and transparent with their employees, labor leaders, even outside suppliers, all in an effort to facilitate effective communication, therefore minimizing the possibility of disconnect within their culture.

Southwest Airlines has consistently received the lowest ratio of complaints per passengers boarded of all major U.S. carriers since such figures began being compiled back in 1987.

It was recognized as one of the Best Places to Work in 2014, a Glassdoor Employees' Choice Award, and was recognized by Chief Executive Group as one of the 2014 Best Companies for Leaders (Southwest Corporate Fact Sheet).

The latest figures released in April 2014 show that the employees of Southwest Airlines will split up $228 million in profit sharing, based on 2013 profitability numbers, in addition to the company's already existing contributions to their 401(k) accounts, medical insurance and health and well-being programs (Maxon 2014). I imagine they are feeling like owners.

Information

Southwest Airlines created a very unique position they call a Boundary Spanner. These people bring together information from different operating units of the business. The ideal Boundary Spanner will build relationships between the different business units of the organization through the shared information. This facilitates the building of working relationships around common goals and mutual respect.

The basic benefits of having such a person in place are multiple. The use of shared information helps others see the bigger picture, which in turn enables them to perform their job more effectively. Because the Boundary Spanner works with employees to build relationships, the employees have a greater sense of shared identity and shared vision. This, in return, raises the collaboration levels where otherwise, the differing interests of the groups could potentially create conflict.

Where most large companies rely on technology to manage information, the Boundary Spanner gives a human face to the process, which builds and strengthens interoffice relationships—computers don't really care about stuff like that (Gittell 2003).

For communication to be effective, we must be sharing enough information that will enable people to successfully complete their assigned task. Everyone is dependent on information to perform their jobs well. The bigger the picture people have of the business and the processes (accomplished through the sharing of information), the more productive they will be. People are very appreciative when they are given opportunities to learn and grow. It makes them feel valuable and therefore, they will create more value. Shared information is fundamental to making people feel like part of the process, which means that it also raises their sense of workplace currency. Sharing information makes them feel a part of the conversation. All these things together equal that they are more engaged in their work. The more engaged your people are, the more invested they are in the business. The more invested they are, the higher the chances they will deliver an extraordinary performance.

Whenever I have been in a managerial position, my learning rate has been twice what it is when I have been an employee. Why? Because as a manager, I am more involved in discussions, typically included in more meetings, have more one-to-one meetings with higher-ups, and I am pulled in to solve more problems. All of these things contribute to a higher pace of learning, as knowledge and information are made available to me more readily. This kind of development raises my currency, making me more valuable to the company. I also feel more valuable so my investment level is much higher.

By nature, I am a problem solver. When I come into new project, I ask a lot of questions not because I am stupid, but because the more information and knowledge I have, the better able I am to solve problems. Rank and file employees would be just as invested if we involved them more in the conversations, and by conversations, I mean the thought processes. This would enable them to solve more problems on their own. Invite your people into the conversation. I realize it may not be practical to drag your staff around with you to every meeting you have in order to expose them to the same scope of information you receive. But you could rotate them through, so each person in your organization can have a measure of exposure. Have synopsis meetings for the group at which you let the one who went to the meeting give the synopsis to the others. Involve your people in problem solving and invite them to give their input on the work processes. Make sure they have a basic framework of information to work from; no one has anything to contribute if they work in a vacuum.

One of my daughters took a position with a local company in our city. She had a decent work ethic, but primarily approached her work as just a job. The company itself was new and in the pains of growing. There were a few struggles on both sides and we learned later that the new owner wasn't sure my daughter was going to work out. It was probably her work ethic that saved her. At the time, we didn't know the owner was thinking in this way; she only recently learned about it in a meeting. But somewhere in the passage of her tenure there, something turned around with my daughter and her boss noticed the change. I asked my daughter if she knew what changed. Here is what she said: "Things turned around for me when they started inviting me to their meetings and I became more engaged in the business itself. It stopped being 'just a job.'" The owner and company managers started inviting her into the conversation; her level of workplace currency went up, she felt like an insider so her investment level escalated and today, they are grooming her for a management position. This could have been a missed opportunity for both parties. Instead, it became a win for both.

Inclusion
I think lack of inclusion is one of the most common failures in corporate America. Inclusion is one of the most fundamental elements in collaboration and in building extraordinary cultures. If you took a survey of your people asking them whether they feel included or excluded, I would gamble that your top performers would all say they feel included

while the rest would say they feel either totally or at least partially excluded. If you actually took a survey, they would feel more included just because you asked their opinion. The real irony is I have watched leaders on one level complain about being excluded from the level above them, only to subject those under them to the same type of exclusion. It is because we are all measuring our own currency against those above us without given consideration to the currency level of those below us.

As we have previously stated a person's sense of value impacts their performance. People come to jobs with differing levels of value. At the risk of stating the obvious, a person's sense of value is heightened if they feel included. Conversely, their sense of value is lessened if they feel excluded. Feeling excluded breeds a sense of uncertainty, as employees question if leaders value them and their contributions. Our culture should cultivate people's sense of value, not kill it. There is a cycle with exclusion where the sense of value is lessened and then performance levels drop; with the decrease in performance comes more exclusion. It takes a very strong, confident employee to overcome this kind of cycle.

People are motivated to do whatever it takes to maintain their own sense of value. Unchecked, people can become very territorial if they feel their place in the company is in danger of being diminished. Exclusion creates insecurity and uncertainty. It goes without saying that this is at the heart of most office politics. A smart leader will consciously make sure that all team members feel a sense of inclusion, therefore making sure that all currency levels remain high. This creates a healthy collaborative culture. If you can find a way to measure your inclusion rates, you could see for yourself a direct correlation with the performance levels.

John Mackey and Raj Sisodia in their book, *Conscious Capitalism,* have this to say: "It is no coincidence that many conscious businesses organize their people into teams. Working in teams creates familiarity and trust and comes naturally to people. It is deeply fulfilling for people to be part of a team, where their contributions are valued and the team encourages them to be creative and make contributions. A well-designed team structure taps into an otherwise dormant source of synergy, so that the whole becomes greater than the sum of the parts. The team culture of sharing and collaboration is not only fundamentally fulfilling to basic human nature, it is also critical for creating excellence in the workplace" (Mackey and Sisodia 2014).

Most of the conflict in your business is rooted in the breakdown of collaboration, which is tied to a breakdown in communication. If communication is breaking down, then there is a lack of shared information. By the nature of these kinds of disconnects, you create inclusion issues for yourself. You can see how all of these fundamental elements are interdependent on each other. The damage done by the lack of collaboration in a culture can be so severe, it surprises me how often leaders let it go unchecked.

When Tim Cook took over Apple, it was a company divided into specialized groups based on whether they worked in hardware, software design, marketing, or finance with little information being communicated between the groups. In a very real sense, the company was being run in the head of Steve Jobs, and he was the only common denominator between the groups. Tim Cook has a different vision for the future of Apple, however, one of collaboration which he views as a "strategic imperative." Here is what he says: "The lines between hardware, software, and services are blurred or are disappearing." Because of the large number of employees at Apple, "The only way you can pull this off is when everyone is working together well. And not just working together well but almost blending together so that you can't tell where people are working anymore, because they are so focused on a great experience that they are not taking functional views of things" (Stone and Satariano 2014). The height of collaboration is not just working together; in Tim Cook's definition there is a "blending together" where the lines of job functions are not distinguishable. If Apple sees the need for collaboration in their culture, a very radically defined collaboration, don't you think for the rest of us it is worth considerable consideration? ∎

CHAPTER FIVE

Competition
The Good, the Bad, and the Ugly

"It is natural for people to both collaborate and compete."
—John Mackey

I t is no accident that I would follow a chapter on collaboration with a chapter on competition. You must first make collaboration the primary core value before you can build healthy and effective competition within your company, otherwise internal competition will quickly undermine the collaborative effort. I can remember my football coach saying whenever we had any internal conflicts among teammates, "Save it for the game Friday night." The same is true in business—save the killer instinct for your outside competitors.

When I was in high school, I went to the neighborhood pool with some of my friends. This particular pool had both a low and high dive. For some reason, we all decided we would learn to do a gainer off the diving board that day. In case you don't know what a gainer is, it's a dive in which the diver leaves the board facing forward, does a back somersault and enters the water feet first. To the amateur like myself the maneuver initially appears to be contrary to the laws of physics and certainly contrary to what conventional wisdom says is safe, but it is a common dive performed for competition.

We all agreed it was smarter (using the loosest definition of that word) to first attempt the dive from the high board, since we would have more space through which to propel ourselves backward from our initial forward jump. The downside to jumping from the high board, however, is that the risk of pain was greater if the feat went badly. One by one we all gave it a try. Every time one of us got closer to successfully completing the dive, the rest of the group became all the more motivated to keep pushing ourselves to accomplish the feat.

Once we all accomplished the jump from the high board, we moved to the low board. To my surprise, right out of the shoot, I did an almost perfect gainer with a tucked flip and a release that sent me straight down into the water feet first. My friends were as surprised as I was and I am not sure I did a better one the rest of the day. Up to that point in my life, the only accomplished dive I had under my belt was a front flip.

Now here we were, one after another, performing our new feat from the low board. If we had not all kept pushing one other to do more and to keep trying, we would not have accomplished anything individually that day. Even when I came back to the pool the next day by myself, I overheard people saying, "There is one of those guys who were doing gainers yesterday." Somehow we had even gained local attention. Though we were all competing with each other to do the dive first and best, we were not competing against each other. In other words, our goal was not the elimination of the other guy, but our competitive spirit brought the individual achievement of each person to a higher level. This is how internal competition should be, with each person raising the other's performance to extraordinary levels. This is the good of competition

An article from CNNMoney.com originally published on November 13, 2013, reported that Microsoft is putting an end to their employee ranking system. The tag line of the article reads, "Microsoft is getting rid of its much-maligned 'stack ranking' method of reviewing employees." According to the article, the system forced managers to rate a certain percentage of workers as underperforming, no matter what. The system went by another name at Microsoft, "rank and yank." The term came from the systems percentage rankings that typically sent the lower performing 10% of employees packing. The "rank and yank" system was first made popular by Jack Welch, former CEO of General Electric, though he called it "differentiation." Let me tell you up front that Jack Welch does not like the name "rank and yank." Actually, he hates it and would not consider it an accurate characterization of his system. While I would agree with Mr. Welch that the term "rank and yank" is probably not a good representation of his basic management approach he calls differentiation, many companies came to use his methods as a means to fire people, sometimes for no other reason than to better their bottom line or to get rid of an employee they just didn't like, based on their own bias. Mr. Welch would acknowledge that there are abuses of his system in American business. Hopefully we will give Mr. Welch a fair shake before we leave this chapter.

Basic differentiation management theory says that 20% of your employees will be top performers, 70% of your employees will be good performers and 10% will be poor performers. It has that Darwinian natural selection feel about it, though Jack Welch would say those percentages are not written in stone. In all fairness to Mr. Welch, he believed performance evaluation was necessary for employee motivation and team building. He holds that people deserve to know where they stand in the organization. He calls this candor, meaning management should not be ambiguous in their evaluations of employees.

Back to the Microsoft story. According to the CNNMoney.com article, Microsoft was scrapping the Welch management evaluation system because they had come to believe that it hampered internal collaboration due to the system's tendency to promote unhealthy competition. In a letter to the employees, Microsoft's head of human resources said the company would end the practice in favor of a new and more flexible system of employee evaluation, intended to encourage better collaboration among employees. Employees had become focused more on outdoing each other, rather than beating the external competition. This is the bad of competition.

Another scathing article on this subject was written by Kurt Eichenwald and published in the August 2012 issue of *Vanity Fair*. In this article, "Microsoft's Lost Decade," Eichenwald says, "Every employee I interviewed said stack ranking was the most destructive process inside Microsoft and drove out untold numbers of employees." In the stack ranking process, employees were given scores based on a 5-point rating system with one being the top score possible. Annual bonuses for each employee were tied directly to the scores. Most of us who have worked in corporate America are familiar with this type of system. The problem is the stacking system made it difficult to reward a broad group of star performers because the system required managers to cap that group at a certain number or percentage.

Then there is the other, related issue of internal competition among managers who had to fight for their employees' rankings. According to an article written in the *New York Times* by Nick Wingfield entitled "Microsoft Abolishes

Employee Evaluation System," another irritation for many employees was that managers had to discuss final rankings for their employees with groups of other managers, many of whom did not necessarily know the employees being graded. In these meetings, pushy and more articulate managers could successfully argue for better rankings for their top performers, while a star employee with a tongue-tied boss might get penalized. Individual performance can easily get lost in that type of currency-eating jungle. As with many great ideas, something that was created to serve and benefit people had become the master and people were now forced to serve the idea. This is the ugly.

By its nature, a competitive environment only focuses on the achievements of the few and passes out the rewards accordingly. Such an environment often times promotes serving self-interest over bringing value to the whole of the company. After all, if I am competing with you, why would I make opportunity for anything that might allow you to increase your workplace currency over my own, thus reducing my chances for promotion and more rewards? I would be more compelled to suppress your efforts and limit your exposure. By its nature this kind of self-interest is contrary to collaboration. A better business model, as demonstrated by Whole Foods, is based on a more equitable work culture founded on collaboration with a corresponding equitable system of shared rewards (Mackey 2014).

A Personal Story
Like almost every person reading this book, I have had my own experiences with performance evaluations. Rarely did it provide any real increase of my sense of personal respect, dignity, value and currency. At my first "real" corporate job working at a bank in Texas, I received my first performance evaluation (at the time I was very green and unfamiliar with

the process). This evaluation system asked supervisors to rank their employees' performance on a scale of one to five, with one being the highest ranking you could achieve and five being the lowest (good chance they were employing the differentiation system of management; at that point, I just had never heard that term). The supervisor completing my review told me that, from her view, you had to walk on water to qualify for a one ranking. Based on that initial statement, I quickly deduced I wasn't going to get a one (though if she had provided the water, I might have attempted it).

In all fairness, I must tell you that this supervisor and I were not the best of friends. I would not have ranked her a one for her job performance either. Nevertheless, there we were evaluating me and with the ranking of one taken out of the picture, that left rankings two through five. I knew the supervisor couldn't very well justify giving me a three or lower because regardless of how she felt about me personally, my job performance was above average. So in the end, my supervisor gave me a ranking of two and a half, which merited a 4% raise—standard for employees in my position. As you might guess, this review process did not spur me on to greater achievement. It did, however, motivate me to look for another position within the bank, hopefully working for someone less likely to be the offspring of Attila the Hun.

Not long after that evaluation, the bank closed that department, giving me the perfect opportunity to move to a different position within the bank. In my new position, I had an interesting exchange with my new supervisor. After only a couple of months in the new department, having quickly become a valued member of the team, my new manager realized the two and a half I had received on my first evaluation was far from accurate. At that time, my new manager confided in me that they almost did not hire me because of the two and a half ranking I had received from my previous supervisor. She felt so strongly about the inaccuracy of my previous review that she got in the face of my previous supervisor and told her that the two and a half ranking she gave me could have cost the bank a valuable employee (or something like that).

How can evaluations be effective if ones are only reserved for those who walk on water? On the other hand, if anything less than a two ranking results in an employee being unable to promote or worse, shown the door, you still have lost any meaningful range of evaluation. How in the world can such a ranking system be useful to anyone—a ranking system in which three of the rankings will cost you your job or at least a promotion? If evaluations are flawed, it is because they become too subjective and leave too much room for bias. Coupled with the understanding that people are motivated differently, your risk of creating employee disconnect through ranking systems many times outweighs the benefits.

If employees feel that a ranking system is unjust and inequitable, it can have a very negative effect on their motivation. Too many employers have the mindset that, in this economy, their employees should just be glad they have a job. We all should be glad we have a job, but is that really what you want to be the sole basis for your employees' motivation? If I had the attitude that I was doing my employer a favor by working for them, they would think me arrogant. But I have worked for managers who acted like they were doing me a favor by employing me. Either way, that relationship is flawed. The success of the employee/employer relationship is based on an exchange of value, with both bringing something to the table. That way everybody holds their head up, no crouching.

Any evaluation system—differentiation or otherwise—should serve to raise the employee's sense of workplace currency, not undermine it. If you study Jack Welch, I believe that is the original intent of his system. However, in my experience, I have not seen rankings raise the motivation of the average employee, elevating his performance to extraordinary levels. The manager may employ candor in his evaluation of the employee's performance, but he often lacks accurate information needed to accurately assess performance or the candor is restricted to only negative feedback.

Workplace Bias

I've mentioned bias before in relation to its effect on perception, but I think bias merits mention again. Bias in the workplace is extremely detrimental when not recognized and checked. It is a bridge for currency if it favors you. It is a battle for currency if it is against you. On the one hand, where the bias is in your favor, currency is given without any real effort required on your part. In contrast, those for whom the bias swings against them have to work twice as hard simply to stay in the game. The emotional energy needed to compensate for bias can be so great that the employee will just eventually disengage and ultimately, disconnect. The negative energy that is produced by bias can be so debilitating that exceptional performance is inhibited, no matter how much talent there may have been. This, of course, perpetuates the bias, creating an unending cycle that is difficult to break. If you have been in that cycle you know it can be exhausting. Bias makes for an unlevel playing field.

Jack Welch makes the statement that the world seems to favor the energetic and the extroverted, in contrast to the shy and introverted. The bias in this statement is obvious, even if unintentional. The pairings of the words imply that everyone who is extroverted is energetic, while everyone who is introverted is timid. Bill Gates of Microsoft and Larry Page of Google both happen to be introverts. Thank goodness for things like the Myers-Briggs test that shows the value of all types of personalities in the workplace!

Stereotypes exist and where bias based on stereotypes exists in the workplace, a certain type of person is given an amount of currency regardless of performance, while the anti-type has to elevate their performance to gain the same amount of currency. On the outside, it may look like the favored type is more productive but in truth, he was given the advantage from the outset which required no investment on his part. Someone under a stereotype bias can find it difficult to compete no matter how hard they work. Bias can be so appearances driven that many people in the workplace get overlooked and development opportunities are not extended so we never see the full potential of those who work for us. A smart leader must make a deliberate decision not to be driven by appearance, but train himself to look past the stereotypes.

I can remember one organization that I wanted to be a part of and felt like I would be a good fit and team player. After being passed over several times, I tried to assess why I had not been chosen for inclusion. If you ask my wife she will tell you that my nature is to be analytical and typically turn the spotlight on myself, to my own detriment. Thinking that something was lacking in me that was keeping me out of the team, one day I heard one of the leadership team members talk about something in his character that needed to change. He had come to realize that he was a controlling person. When I heard that, I realized this was true to some degree or another in all the leaders in that organization, including those who made the hiring decisions. I then realized that even if it was inadvertent, they made a habit of hiring leaders who all had this characteristic. They were assessing controlling-type personalities as a good leadership indicator, wrongly equating it with confidence. I have had my own issues to work though, but being controlling is not one of them. I came to recognize the bias, that they were hiring people just like themselves. Employees can recognize bias in the workplace. They can recognize when the odds are stacked against them, limiting any chance they have for advancement.

A Closer Look at Differentiation

To determine if there is a place for evaluation, let's walk through Jack Welch's justification for his differentiation doctrine. I'm using Jack Welch's own words, taken from an article he wrote for the *Wall Street Journal* on November 14, 2013, which I feel lays out his basic beliefs on the subject of employee evaluation. The article was written in response to the 2013 Microsoft announcement that the company would be dropping their "rank and yank" evaluation practice, which was based on Jack Welch's differentiation paradigm.

Should evaluations be used by companies as a tool to identify their weak performers in order to eliminate them? Jack says, "Unlike 'rank and yank'—I hate even using that term—differentiation isn't about corporate plots, secrecy or purges. It's about building great teams and great companies through consistency, transparency and candor." Evaluations are an appropriate tool if they are used with the right motives and the right goals. The purpose of evaluation must be to raise motivation, increase workplace currency, and not break people down or debilitate them. This can be something as simple as saying, "These are the things I see that are really great. This is what I want to see more of." Generalities tend to be useless. Before candor can be an effective tool, time is needed to build relationships and establish trust.

Is evaluation an effective tool for measuring performance? Jack Welch says differentiation is "about aligning performance with the organization's missions and values. Differentiation starts with communication, exhaustive communication of a company's mission and its values." Mr. Welch puts the responsibility on leaders to communicate mission and values; he uses terms such as "specific," "granular," and "vivid" on how the vision should be communicated. We have talked about vision and how important it is that employees are connected to it and how vision can impact performance.

Like at Microsoft, evaluations can become about measuring employees against each other. Because the rankings are tied to money and promotion, the system quickly deteriorates into the business of undermining your fellow employee, if for no other reason than for survival. One team member should not feel they have to diminish another to maintain or raise their own currency level. According to my research, this is the exact thing Microsoft was experiencing and it became a cancer that ate away at their culture.

According to the Welch way, evaluation is about measuring an employee's performance against the expressed mission and values of the company, after considerable effort has been given to the "exhaustive" (Mr. Welch's word) communication of its content. This kind of evaluation with an emphasis on preemptive communication of the unifying purpose of the company is much more collaborative in nature than competitive. The reality too often is that communication of the company's mission and core values is extremely weak and in direct correlation, the levels of employee motivation and performance are also weak. The problem is, at evaluation time, the responsibility for lack of motivation and for poor performance is solely placed on the employee. Smart leaders understand performance is a shared responsibility between management and employee. Evaluations are a good opportunity to assess if the employee is connecting with the company vision and core values. That tends to be a source of performance issues more than anything else.

This raises a second question: Are evaluations just about quantitative results? I remember one owner telling one of his very hard-working employees how he hated paying people who don't generate revenue. This particular employee who was putting his heart and soul into the business happened to fall into that category (an erroneous category) because of the supportive nature of their job. That's a case study for how to demotivate an already motivated employee. Did he say that for real? Yes, he did, to his face!

What this leader had failed to recognize is even though this employee was not on the front lines of the commission-based part of the business, the organizational talents of this employee were freeing up those front line employees to attend to more customers, enabling them to produce more revenue. He made sure the salespeople had the tools and supplies they needed to service the customers, therefore impacting client satisfaction, which meant repeat business. The employee's performance was not quantitative in terms of actual numbers but qualitative in terms of supporting others, helping them to produce. In addition, he was advancing the objectives of the company vision and having an equal impact on the company's numbers by raising customer satisfaction and repeat business. That is money in the bank.

Jack Welch says, "Yes, the system looks at quantitative results … but it also looks just as carefully at behaviors, the qualitative factors." The performance of the aforementioned employee could only be measured qualitatively in their organization skills, in their service mindset toward their fellow workers and the advancement of the core values of the company. Everything cannot be measured simply in numbers.

Is evaluation a good tool for letting people know where they stand? Mr. Welch says, "Another criticism of differentiation is that it requires managers to let every employee know where he or she stands—how they're doing today, both quantitatively and qualitatively, and what their future with the company looks like." In the Welch system, there are the stars in terms of both results and values (in the top 20% of the team), those who are about average (about 70%), and those not up to expectations (the bottom 10%). In his view, a manager owes candor to their people so that they are not guessing about what the organization thinks of them in terms of what percentage group they fall in.

Here is where I agree with Mr. Welch in principle, but the system more often fails in practice. People need to know where they stand in terms of how they are valued in the company. Since performance is tied to the person's sense of value, candor is only effective if it is increasing their sense of currency in the workplace, not diminishing it. Too many managers are not skilled enough communicators to be effective when speaking candidly. Trust must first be established before candid comments can be constructive. This requires time and effort to build such a relationship. Based on interviews I have seen with Mr. Welch, I do not think he would disagree.

Is evaluation an effective tool for mentoring? According to Mr. Welch, the components that make differentiation work so effectively are feedback and coaching: "Your stars know they are loved and rarely leave. Those in the middle 70% know that they are appreciated and they receive clear guidance about how to improve their performance. And the bottom 10% is never surprised when the conversation sometimes turns, after a year of candid appraisals, to moving on."

I believe evaluation could be a great tool for mentoring, but my experience has been that many managers don't have the needed coaching skills to help their employees move to the next level in their performance, nor are they able to provide significant feedback. In some instances, leaders become testy when just asked a simple question. Question and answer is a major component of effective mentoring. If Rainmaker is right and nine out of ten managers are under managing, it is unlikely any real mentoring is going on from the top down.

I have experience from one end of the spectrum to the other. I've had a manager who didn't really want to fill out the evaluation, but did it just so she could give me a raise (which I did appreciate). On the other hand, I've had a manager who really couldn't find anything constructive to say but still put a negative comment on my evaluation based on one isolated incident that occurred one day out of the 365 days of the year. That one negative comment did not reflect the whole of my annual performance or accurately attest to what actually happened.

Though I received a raise from the first manager, her failure to provide me with any quantitative or qualitative feedback about my performance made the evaluation very generic. My main concern is what assessment other managers would make who might look into my file. The worst part is my job at that time was very quantitative and could have been easily measured.

The danger of evaluations is if you are not accurately assessing your employees, you are running a high risk of negatively impacting their motivation and decreasing their sense of currency. In return, the evaluation is having a negative impact on performance instead of bringing about the desired improvement. Instead of building trust, it is eroding it because your employees are thinking to themselves, "This manager has no clue who I am or what I can do." You can't trust someone if you feel they have not put in the time to formulate an accurate assessment of your abilities. If leaders are going to provide effective feedback (candor) and coaching, they must put forth the effort to get to know those who work for them. This takes a measure of concentrated time and observation, which many managers would say their busy schedule does not allow. The Rainmaker report found that productivity and quality improve almost immediately when leaders begin spending time in regular dialogues with their people providing the basic management basics we just talked about.

There is nothing as motivating as a manager pointing out something positive they see in your performance. It makes you say to yourself, "Wow, they are paying attention." Now that is a trust builder, not a trust buster. The right kind of feedback should build connection that is a characteristic of an effective coach. Employees want to know that you "get" them.

Collaborating and connecting cultures have more impact on performance and production than anything else. Like Microsoft, evaluate your culture and determine if there are any values being promoted that are detrimental to a climate of collaboration. The widespread corporate benefit of that evaluation will be greater than anything a single employee evaluation will ever produce.

The story of my friends and me at the pool that I told at the beginning of this chapter is an example of how competition and collaboration can work together. My friends and I were pursuing the same common objective, while also challenging each other to achieve more. We were all working toward the same goal and our competition served as fuel to propel us all to a higher level of achievement. Yes, this was a story from my childhood, but then again, the Jack Welch idea of differentiation is based in the childhood practice of picking teams on the playground. In that scenario, the supposed best players are picked first while the rest of the group is left feeling somewhat excluded and dejected. Personally, I like my story better. ▪

CHAPTER SIX

Engagement
Understanding Workplace Currency

"A company can grow big without losing the passion and personality that built it, but only if it's driven not by profits but by people."

—Howard Schultz

What most research companies agree on is the percentage of employees who are disengaged. Their numbers are all roughly the same, reporting that around 70% of American workers are disengaged at their job. As available and accessible as this knowledge is, I was still surprised that the number is so high and that business leaders are not attacking this problem more aggressively. If you compare those numbers with the numbers advocated by the Jack Welch differentiation philosophy where 20% are top performers, 10% are underperformers and 70% are average or above, it might lead one to think there are some parallels.

Apparently this undefined, disengaged 70% are still able

to perform their jobs well enough to stay out of the unemployment line. Let us consider for a moment that maybe the
reason they are disengaged is because they are not "feeling
the love" that the Welch 20% are being shown. I know what
you're thinking: "What's love got to do with it?"

Workplace Currency

I introduced the idea of workplace currency at the beginning
of this book. Workplace currency is simply our sense of our
personal value in the workplace. It is also tied to how much
value we feel we are bringing to the workplace. When we start
a job, we come to work with both of those dynamics in play,
giving us a sense of currency in our workplace, and the workplace can either positively or negatively impact it. There is a
direct correlation between the level of workplace currency an
employee feels they have and their level of engagement. Their
level of engagement will determine their level of performance.

In Jack Welch's world of differentiation here is what he says
about the 20%: "The top 20 percent of employees are show-
ered with bonuses, stock options, praise, love, training, and
a variety of rewards to their pocketbooks and souls. There
can be no mistaking the stars at a company that differenti-
ates. They are the best and are treated that way." Mr. Welch
understands he must keep his top 20% engaged by keeping
their sense of value elevated, ensuring they have plenty of
workplace currency. That's the love.

Here is what Mr. Welch says about the 70%: "The middle 70 percent are managed differently. This group of people
is enormously valuable to any company; you simply cannot
function without their skills, energy, and commitment. After
all, they are the majority of your employees. And that's the
major challenge, and risk, in 20-70-10—keeping the middle
70 engaged and motivated." My goal here is not to take Mr.
Welch to task, not that I could or would. But his own words

help make my point. Why do we think the middle 70% have to be managed differently? Are they motivated differently? Are their needs not the same? The answer is yes; they are enormously valuable and need the same kinds of workplace currency to stay engaged. The 70% are disengaged because they know they are treated differently. They are told they are valuable, but they don't see the words backed up by the actions needed to fulfill their own need for workplace currency and sense of value. Their engagement, therefore, is commensurate with the level of currency they have been given. In many cases, the workplace is lowering their sense of currency. If their currency is dropping, can you guess what else is dropping with it? Their performance, in that they are giving you just enough to keep themselves employed. I said they were disengaged, not stupid.

Culture sets the expectations for what people feel they need to do to earn workplace currency. A culture of differentiation can set the expectation that higher levels of currency are at the top 20%. To be in the 70% becomes less desirable because of the limited amount of currency that can be attained. Eventually after a prolonged period of time, motivation is weakened and employees become disengaged. It is not that the 70% expect everything to be equal. It is the disproportionate amount of currency that is awarded without basis. It is not my intent to make currency all about money, except that it does represent value and is the easiest example to use to illustrate the point. Let's look at what John Mackey and Raj Sisodia say about this in *Conscious Capitalism:*

> *"Top executives at the helm of many major corporations have rigged the game to enrich themselves at the expense of the company and its stakeholders. According to the Institute for Policy Studies, the ratio between CEO pay and average pay was 42:1 in 1980, 107:1 in 1990, and*

525:1 in 2000. It has fluctuated in recent years, standing at 325:1 in 2010."

It is not that the expectation is that CEO pay should not be higher; it is the disproportionate amount that is troubling. Mackey and Sisodia set forth "conscious" alternatives to this trend. First, they advocate Stakeholder Integration, which simply means, "Conscious businesses recognize that each of their stakeholders is important and all are connected and interdependent, and that the business must seek to optimize value creation for all of them. All the stakeholders of a conscious business are motivated by a shared sense of purpose and core values." What they are calling value creation is similar to what I refer to as workplace currency. Money is involved because it represents value, but value creation is not limited to just money. We cannot deny that compensation can lower someone's sense of currency and be a reason they would disengage if they thought it was not equitable.

Let's look at another trend identified by Mackey and Sisodia: "The second stakeholder cancer threat comes from *senior management teams* that seek to maximize their own compensation without creating commensurate value. In many cases, executives simply pay themselves too much, with little concern for internal equity or connection with overall performance." Okay, this is more about money, but let's substitute the broader idea of currency for the word compensation. In the workplace, when higher levels of currency are given and there is no creation of "commensurate value," it creates an imbalance. It impacts the internal equity of the culture and causes those who are getting the short end to disengage.

My biggest complaint with a management system like differentiation is that it is self-perpetuating. Considering the amount of currency given to the 20%, whether it be in the form of bonuses, stock options, praise, love, training, and a variety of rewards to their pocketbooks and souls—all are types of currency—they continue to be highly motivated and perform at levels commensurate with the currency they receive and so retain their position at the top. Those in the 70% who must perform at the same level to make it into the 20%, but who do not enjoy the same level of currency, find it more difficult to break the barrier. Therefore, differentiation can become a system that self-perpetuates its own numbers, even as those numbers are used to justify its viability. Let us take a closer look at the non-monetary face of currency.

Value

If we feel valuable, we are more creative, innovative and productive. Our level of currency at work elevates those feelings of being valuable. Value is the baseline of currency. People bring to work different levels of their own sense of value depending on their background, upbringing and life experiences. What leaders should understand is it takes just as much effort to raise someone's sense of value as it does to destroy it. Even if you're a bottom line type of leader and not so inclined to pay attention to what you perceive as the "touchy-feely" parts of management, you must understand that making your employees feel valuable will pay off with higher levels of performance. Ralph Waldo Emerson said, "Treat a man as he is, and he will remain as he is. Treat a man as he could be, and he will become what he should be." The 20% continue as the top 20% because their performance is reinforced with workplace currency. How do you motivate the 70% to higher levels of performance and keep them engaged? In the same way as you do the 20%. Keep their sense of value high.

Development

Development should be offered at every level of your organization. This topic is so important, I dedicated the whole next chapter to it, but because it is so much a part of currency, I need to mention it here. Development raises currency. You would be surprised how sharply your employees' performance will rise by just raising their information and knowledge level. The worst offense of the command and control type of manager is the withholding of information and knowledge. The main reason it is withheld is because of the perceived threat an informed workforce brings to a system of hierarchal control. It is simply a power play move.

Google rejected the top down hierarchy style of leadership. Instead, they use a strategy of Iterate and Co-create. This gives the collective intelligence of the entire organization a voice and access to available information. In simple terms, they have invited the whole company to join the conversation. It is like a blank check of workplace currency given to the entire company.

Recognition

Recognition is the biggest part of currency. We all need recognition to progress in our careers and in our development. The difficult part is balancing a team-oriented collaborative effort with individual recognition. You must have both dynamics to have a successful culture that cultivates exceptional performance. If you have a culture where people have to fight for recognition, then you create the unhealthy competitive culture that undermines the collaborative effort.

Leaders must keep favoritism in check. We all have a tendency to promote our favorites. The underlying premise of a team is that each member is capable of bringing something of value to the table, contributing to the success of the whole. But each member needs recognition and reward for their contribution. If one member feels like they have to fight for recognition, they appear confrontational and it looks like they are not a team player. Smart leaders make sure individual recognition is correctly distributed. We must give credit where credit is due. This eliminates unnecessary conflict between team members because they are not fighting with each other over currency. Because favorites tend to get credit easily, leaders have to be intentional in giving recognition to all.

Let me just note, if you as a leader feel competitive toward one of your team members, you will tend to discount their ideas and only give credit to the team, disregarding their individual contribution. Because recognition is so central to motivation and impacts an employee's opportunities to be promoted, it is important we get this right. You create all kinds of disconnect issues if you're in a currency battle with the people who work for you.

Control

John Mackey says conscious managers exercise a minimal amount of control. Their role is not to control other people; it is to create the conditions that allow for more self-management. How much control a person feels they have over their job directly correlates to the amount of workplace currency they feel they possess. The more control, the higher the currency. If you have someone who has the capability to self-direct their own efforts, by micromanaging them, you are cheating yourself, the employee and the company. Micromanagement almost always has a negative impact on performance. As performance suffers, the tendency is to increase the micromanagement. This creates a downward spiral that will end in frustration for everyone, and the employee will ultimately disengage. The real source of the problem is not the employee's performance, though that will be the most likely conclusion. The truth is, people who are at liberty to self-direct are much more engaged.

There is nothing more positively potent to human motivation than to have a sense of control over your life and future, and nothing is as detrimental as to feel you have no control at all. Self-directed people know the right questions to ask if they are given the right information up front about their objective and how to use upper management as a resource and report on their own progress.

We have talked about Google how they have a very flat, non-hierarchal culture where everyone has nearly the same equality. It is an equality that is based on the value of an idea, not on how long you have been there or how high up you are in the organization. Employees are able to work on their own terms and managers are viewed as leaders who support their work, not as bosses who dictate their tasks. Twenty percent of their time can be dedicated solely to their own pursuits (Reck).

A series of studies called the Whitehall Studies were conducted in Great Britain. The first study took place over a series of years in the late 1960s; the second took place over a series of years in the mid to late 1980s. The studies sought to determine the link between socioeconomic level and stress as they followed a large number of civil servants, tracking their jobs levels, social habits, and overall health. One of the most interesting things they found was that there is a direct correlation between how much perceived control you have over your job and how much stress you experience. Those employees who felt they had little control over their jobs experienced higher levels of stress. This, in turn, impacted their health. This seems contrary to what you would believe to be true. Often we equate higher levels of responsibility with higher stress levels. But the reality is, giving an employee a sense of control over their own job, a sense of ownership over what they do, makes for a more productive, innovative, happier and healthier employee (Marmot 2002). I would bet they are more engaged as well.

Why They Are Disengaged

These same research companies who uncovered the percentages of disengaged workers also agree that the answer to this question of engagement lies somewhere in leadership. Why blame the leadership? Because it makes no sense to blame those who historically have had the least amount of control over their own jobs in the traditional hierarchal workplace. I am talking about the employee. As leaders, we either increase the opportunity for procurement of workplace currency through value, recognition, development and control or we restrict it. We set in place the culture that determines how currency is obtained and distributed.

Google has one manager for every thirty people. For their culture, this greatly reduces the possibility for micromanagement. Employees view their managers not as the people in charge, but as resources to help facilitate their individual performance and achievement. Engagement is, to a great degree, dependent on the leadership and their ability to create a culture that provides the many faces of currency.

Workplace Bias and Its Impact on Engagement

I have talked about workplace bias previously in a different context. Because I think it has such tremendous impact on employee engagement, I want to revisit the idea here.

We all must deal with our bias. This is part of our own developmental process. Maybe your initial reaction to that statement is to claim that you don't have any bias. That reaction is the surest indicator that you most likely do have a bias; probably more than one

If we look at a bias in its simplest form as something that influences or colors our thinking in a certain way, then we should admit we all have bias in some form or another. Let me help you out with this one. The first bias we all should admit to is we think everyone else should be just like us and do things the same way as us. Keep in mind that if you continue to proclaim your innocence in this area, you will never be free of your bias that is causing damage to others in the workplace. Here is what I mean. If we acknowledge that it is possible that we have a bias, it is more likely we will look at ourselves more closely. As I have said before, self-evaluation is an important leadership quality. In order to be objective toward another, we must first be objective about ourselves. We must ask the question when we are making decisions, giving evaluations or hiring people, "How objectively am I looking at this person or decision?"

From a practical standpoint, I think it is advisable to bring in a peer or two when seeking to make objective decisions about others in the workplace, especially about those who work directly for you. But don't just grab people who think like you; chances are they have the same biases. In some cases, an outside third person can increase the chances of greater objectivity. The old saying that a three-strand cord is not easily broken would be well applied here. Bringing in others to increase objectivity can be especially difficult to put into practice for bully-type leaders who are used to getting their own way, as they are opening themselves up to the thoughts and idea of others. They prefer the deck to be stacked in their favor.

When people come up against bias in the workplace, it can be frustrating, debilitating and result in disengagement. If an employee does not think the work culture is objective and equitable and repeatedly comes up against a bias, he will eventually lose heart and give up. Bias creates a cycle that feeds on itself because it sets out to prove itself to be true. If not identified and dealt with, it can be very devastating to a company's culture. The mark of this kind of culture is a low retention rate and high turnover.

Biased-based evaluations have immediate impact on the

lives of people and can directly affect their engagement in their job. As leaders, we have an obligation to maintain a high level of objectivity. But maintaining objectivity does not come naturally and requires a conscious deliberate choice to evaluate our decisions and continually check ourselves for any trace of bias.

In summary, disengagement is no big mystery; the disengaged are not "feeling the love" and so are forced to look for it elsewhere. If it is true that people leave managers, not companies, it is because a manager did not provide an appropriate level of currency and created a disconnect. People are wired to be engaged and if Daniel Pink is right, their intrinsic drivers will move them to find a place they will be. Low levels of currency cripple employee motivation and performance. As leaders, we want to do things that raise the currency levels of our people. This is a key to exceptional and engaging cultures. Having currency is basic to human motivation. When it is low, people see themselves as only having a job and they will think that is all you expect from them. ∎

CHAPTER 7

Development
Your Best Investment

*"Before you are a leader, success is all about growing yourself.
When you become a leader, success is all about growing others."*
—Jack Welch

*"The conventional definition of management is getting work
done through people, but real management is developing
people through work."*
—Agha Hasan Abedi

I have an older brother who owns a lake house on a very popular lake in our state. He also owns a boat and he often invites our family out to enjoy both his lake house and boat. When we go out on the boat, I always offer to help with some of the tasks associated with going out on the water, but my brother usually insists on doing things himself. He owns one of those inflatable rafts called a Mable that you can attach to a rope and pull behind the boat. I have offered on several occasions to attach the rope to the boat but I always get the same response from him: "I'll get it." After getting the same answer on all those occasions, I decided to stop offering to help. It is his boat so it's his call. Besides, I love my brother so it really doesn't matter. I resigned myself to be a spectator.

One day we were out in the boat, my brother's wife was on their Sea-Doo, and we were pulling the kids on the Mable that was attached to the back of the boat. I had been watching the kids and happened to glance around to the front of the boat just in time to see a wave catch the front of the Sea-Doo and push my brother's wife off the back. The moment was a little surreal, like when your mind doesn't click with what your eyes just saw. The Sea-Doo is designed to shut off if the rider is thrown from the craft, as the key is attached to the rider's life jacket. But in this case, the key somehow came loose from the life jacket and remained in the ignition, so the Sea-Doo kept going without its rider.

I quickly alerted my brother to the situation and he responded with a mix of unbelief and alarm as he spotted the still moving Sea-Doo, now missing his wife. He yelled back at me to untie the Mable that was carrying two of my children so we could pursue the Sea-Doo unhindered. They would be safe on the Mable until we came back for them. The problem was that I had never tied on the Mable, so my attempts to untie it in that moment of crisis were sluggishly unsuccessful. Of course, my brother was somewhat irritated by my lack of progress, mainly because of the stress he was under. He kept yelling at me to hurry up and I yelled back that I didn't know how to untie the rope. With that response, he came back and untied the Mable himself. Once the Mable was loose, we were able to retrieve the moving Sea-Doo and my brother's wife. The crisis was averted.

Once the crisis was over my brother said, "I guess I never showed you how to tie the Mable to the boat, so I couldn't really expect you to know how to untie it." If I would have had more time, I could have eventually figured out how to free the Mable from the boat, but in the moment of crisis, time was something we didn't have. I have observed leaders run their business just this same way. They insist on doing so much of the work themselves, their employees only know enough to do the task they have been assigned but not much more. Of course, the leader claims he doesn't have time to teach anyone the things he is doing, which perpetuates the notion that only he can be trusted with the bigger pieces of the business. The leader then feels that he carries all the weight and no one knows what it's like to be him and no one really appreciates how much he does. When anyone dares to disagree with how he is doing things, he proceeds to put that person in his place by degrading or demoralizing them in some way. Truth be told, it is far easier to keep undeveloped employees in their place.

This is a sure way to set your employees up to fail. Most leaders don't come to the realization that my brother did— that his initial expectation for me to untie the Mable was misplaced and unfair. By never teaching me how to tie the Mable and never giving me the opportunity to actually do it, he set me up to fail in the time of crisis. And in crisis, he could not efficiently handle all that had to be done.

Whether such behavior is rooted in a control issue or a power trip or just a lack of basic trust in other people, it places a lid on the development of employees and severely limits the ability of the company to grow. The problem with this style of leadership is when there is a crisis and the leader is barking orders, he can't understand why no one can perform tasks outside of their norm fast enough or with any kind of accuracy. These types of scenarios seem to reinforce the underlying belief that the leader is the only one who can really get things done. Adding insult to injury, the employees usually take the blame for the failed production, creating an obvious disconnect.

The secret to successfully managing a crisis is to develop your team before the crisis comes. If your communication is not good when things are normal, it will not improve in the midst of a crisis. If collaboration, the one thing you will desperately need in a difficult situation, has not been a core value of your company, then your business will crumble under the weight of a crisis. One of the tragedies of the *Titanic* is that little time was given to allow the crew to practice the evacuation of the ship. The assumption was it would never be needed.

The fast and furious leadership style will often ignore or forego employee development because it is viewed as an impediment to reaching the desired goal. The lack of attention to developmental needs will actually work against reaching the goal, but the leader failures to recognize this truth, causing him to simply push his employees harder. In some cases, questions from employees are viewed as something else just slowing down progress, so development suffers further. This kind of leader is usually very smart, which adds to the challenge of showing them the errors in their leadership style. Daniel Goleman in his book *Primal Leadership* calls this type of leader a "pacesetter." Pacesetters are not without merit in that they challenge and set exciting goals for people, but their management style can also have a negative impact on culture in their efforts to sustain the fast and furious pace (Goleman 2013).

Howard Schultz, in his book *Pour Your Heart Into It: How Starbucks Built a Company One Cup at a Time,* says, "When companies fail, or fail to grow, it's almost always because they don't invest in the people, the systems, and the processes they need" (Schultz 1997). A badly managed crisis is only revealing that you have failed to properly develop your people and your culture.

In *Onward,* Howard Schultz recounts the Starbucks crisis

of 2007. The crisis would prompt his return as CEO in 2008. According to Shultz, Starbucks had begun a downward spiral "failing itself." The problem was rooted in an obsession for growth measured by numbers. With such high-speed growth, it became difficult to meet the demand for opening new stores without shortcutting the proper training of new employees and newly promoted managers. This was costing Starbucks their culture. Schultz recounts: "Our turnover rates in stores were too high, and a new generation of baristas had not been effectively trained or inspired by Starbucks' mission."

His solution, at the cost of millions of dollars to the company and at the risk of their public image, was to shut down all the stores in the U.S. and retrain the baristas. He believed by providing them with more tools and knowledge, he would improve their work experience as well as the customers' experience. (Schultz 2011)

We will all face a crisis at one time or another. Managing a crisis has more to do with maintaining the core strategies and values you have established before the crisis comes. In Starbucks' case, they had lost sight of their core strategies and values and it had an adverse effect on employee development.

Smart leaders know the importance of developing their people so as to have an efficient, knowledgeable team that can carry out what is needed, even in a crisis. Smart leaders see the value in their people and know that by providing the right tools and training, their people can deliver an extraordinary performance and handle a crisis or, in many cases, avert a crisis altogether. You will even discover they can do some things better than you. In those moments, smart leaders don't "push back" or discount and are glad to allow their people to excel. Dream teams are not just a result of finding the right people, but by creating the right culture where the right people can develop to their full potential.

Feedback and Development

One of the easiest methods to promote development can be found within the day-to-day interactions. I emphasized earlier how important it is to invite employees to enter the conversation. Part of that conversation is allowing employee feedback in the form of questions, observations and assessments. This is one of the best ways to not only promote team building but to raise the levels of innovation, creativity and process improvements.

I was working at a company where I was a minority shareholder and a board member. It was a small business fewer than 50 employees. The majority shareholder wanted to hire a certain individual for a position in our company that required good people skills. The individual he had found currently worked as a contractor's helper on his residence. The potential new hire was brought to the office for an interview, but another board member and I were left out of the interview process.

After the interview, one of the board members who was in the interview brought the candidate over for me to meet him. Now what I knew of him before our conversation was that he had previously worked around but not directly in the type of work for which he was being hired. But what I didn't know was whether his previous work experience required any of the needed people skills that would be required in his new position. My suspicions were it did not. I asked one simple question: Did he have any interaction with people in the course of his previous jobs? Turns out, he had only worked as a manual laborer and had no experience talking to people. Based on that answer, I was confident this man did not have the people skills necessary to do the job for which we wanted to hire him.

After the candidate left, we gathered together as a board to vote on this possible hire. I voiced my concern over this person's lack of people skills needed to do the job. Not having been invited to take part in the initial interview, I was assured by the primary and secondary owners of the company who were in the interview that the man was the right person for the job.

Three months after we hired the man, the primary owner announced at a board meeting that they were letting the gentleman go because he did not have the people skills necessary to do the job. Had the owner heeded the advice of those around him, the company could have been saved three months of wasted resources and from putting this individual in the unemployment line, who had left another job to take this one—a disservice to both our company and him. Not only was I left out of the interview, but my feedback was discounted, though it proved to be an accurate assessment.

A smart leader knows where he is weak and where he needs others to fill the gaps. He lets others function in their strengths and bring their gifts, talents or skills to the forefront. Howard Schultz said it this way: "Early on I realized that I had to hire people smarter and more qualified than I was in a number of different fields, and I had to let go of a lot of decision-making. I can't tell you how hard that is. But if you've imprinted your values on the people around you, you can dare to trust them to make the right moves" (Schultz 1997). We as leaders need to recognize that no one person is the best at everything, that we need other people to fill those gaps.

Smart leaders are not bent on showing that they are the smartest people in the room. Their focus is instead on helping other people feel smarter. Some leaders think that making other people feel inferior somehow builds character or something stupid like that. If people are inhibited to share ideas with you, it is likely because you quickly discount them. This type of behavior can single-handedly crush the very thing you should be promoting—feedback. Feedback is an essential building block to collaboration and to building extraordinary teams.

I have known people who had extremely smart business minds, but who were somewhat stupid when it came to knowing how to manage people. I remember hearing a leader boast about how he had never read a book on management. I didn't really have the heart to tell him how badly it showed.

Smart leaders are not arrogant; they have humility. That doesn't make them weak. Quite the opposite, arrogance shows weakness because it is based in insecurity. How do you distinguish between arrogance and confidence? Confident leaders do not need to discount other people. Discounting is based in insecurity.

Smart leaders are characterized by how they listen and respond to those they lead. Smart leaders are always pushing you to be better, to be more than what you currently are. Smart leaders see the future potential in their people, not just what they are seeing in today's performance. If not, how can they possibly hope to lead them to higher levels of performance? How can they hope to motivate them? By definition, to motivate is to move something forward. How can you move someone forward if you can't see them beyond where they are today? This is at the heart of development—it is not "today" focused; it is "tomorrow" focused. You develop today for tomorrow's needs. To neglect this is shortsighted.

I can't tell you how many times as a young man I was looking for a leader who could see me further down the road than I could see myself. This was part of the leadership voice in my own life. I finally just had to find my own inner motivation to move myself forward. Even sometimes today, I find myself pushing against the lids people want to put on my life, wanting to loudly say "get out of my way."

I remember a pastor of a church we attended. One of his

daughters married a young man who also had ministry ambitions. Not too long after the young man and the pastor's daughter were married, he began to preach on Wednesday nights. In the beginning, he performed as you would expect from a young man just starting out, a little rough around the edges. We endured his teaching in the beginning but as he continued, he got better and developed into quite a good preacher over the years. The great opportunity his father-in-law afforded him allowed him to develop in both his skill and his delivery. I thought this was a smart leader practice, but I was troubled the pastor had not done this kind of thing for anyone else, to my knowledge. The tragedy, in my mind, was that he could have possibly done that for 20, maybe 30, even 50 more young men over the lifetime of his ministry. He could have left a legacy of so many more.

What does it mean to lead? I believe it means to take people places they didn't think possible, to give them opportunities to develop their potential. This kind of leadership inspires people and even if the employee eventually moves on to something else for the right reasons—maybe even to something that supersedes the leader's own achievements—they will always point to that person who inspired them as one of their greatest leaders.

One of the most interesting parts of Malcolm Gladwell's book *Outliers* is the research that discovered the majority of birthdays of the elite group of players in the Canadian Hockey League fall in the first quarter of the year, the highest number of players in January (Gladwell 2008). This can be attributed to the fact that the eligibility cutoff date for age class hockey has always been set at January 1. Those whose birthdays fall in January enjoy a full twelve-month maturity advantage over those whose birthdays fall in the latter part of the same year. The coaches, when selecting all-star teams, typically pick the bigger, more coordinated players, assuming they are the more talented. The result being that these players receive better coaching and play fifty to seventy-five games, in contrast to the twenty-five games played by the others. The all-stars also practice two to three times more than the non–all stars. Gladwell points out that by age thirteen and fourteen, with all that extra coaching and practice, they are the better players who go on to make the Major Junior Leagues (Gladwell 2008).

Here is a group of hockey players who, because of when their birthdays fell, enjoyed a size advantage over others in their age group, which won them additional attention and developmental opportunities, leading them to become the elite players. What had they done to earn these advantages? Nothing besides just showing up. Their birthdays simply fell at advantageous times. How many more players could have been stars if they had been given the same developmental opportunities?

To unlock the human potential in anyone requires the opportunity for development. As leaders, we should make that opportunity as all-encompassing as possible and not let favoritism, bias or status restrict it. Nothing provides the opportunity to raise currency more than development. It is a win for all, without even saying what it does for our motivation! ▪

CHAPTER EIGHT

Motivation
Don't Mess It Up

"Outstanding leaders go out of their way to boost the self-esteem of their personnel. If people believe in themselves, it's amazing what they can accomplish."

—Sam Walton

"When you're part of figuring something out, you have much more invested in it."

—Eileen Fisher

The importance of employee engagement is found in its relationship to motivation. If engagement is low, then motivation levels suffer as well. I think we will all agree that performance is driven by motivation. Highly motivated people perform at higher levels. That being said, we should stipulate that we are not creating motivation; we are simply increasing it or decreasing it. The significance of culture is that it is impacting which way the levels of motivation are moving. Everything we have talked about up to this point concerning workplace currency affects motivation.

A Personal Story of the Loss of Motivation

In my early years, I can remember when I was experiencing some disconnect with my immediate supervisor at the bank. He, of course, identified me as the problem. From what I could piece together, he went to our manager and on her advice, had a sit-down with me to discuss what was expected of me, something I was not really confused about in the first place. What he didn't realize is the disconnect had resulted from his own actions toward me in the six months leading up to that conversation, not any confusion on my part concerning expectations.

I had been in that position for two years and up to that point, I had been highly motivated, engaged and had proved my value. My strategy had been simple, to make him look good thinking that in return, he would do the same for me. For those first two years it worked like a charm and we got on quite well. Sometime after that, he had fallen ill with some unusual virus that took him out of the workplace for six to eight weeks. During that time, I reported directly to our manager. This afforded me the opportunity to showcase my abilities without having them filtered through my supervisor. It was like giving someone their first taste of sugar, intoxicating! When my supervisor did come back, he found that my currency levels had been generously raised. So much so that our manager was heralding my management aptitude. At first, this did not create an immediate problem between me and my supervisor. In fact, there was a supervisory position getting ready to open up on the other side of the room for which our manager thought I would be the perfect candidate. However, a decision was made by upper management to dissolve that unit, closing the door on that opportunity.

Not too long after, our manager was moved to a different department. Things then began to change in the thinking of my supervisor toward me. Somehow I had become, in his mind, a threat to his currency and I presume that out of a sense of self-preservation, he started acting very differently toward me. The first thing I noticed was that he immediately began blocking me from access to our new manager. The second thing I noticed was that he started leaving me out of meetings. This put me at a distinct disadvantage within the company. I was young and my first response was to not care, but eventually his actions affected my motivation and I started to disengage. I attempted to change positions within the bank, only to learn later that he was bad mouthing me behind my back, depriving me of any good referrals I would need to secure another position. The damage had been done. He had limited my mobility within the company.

The disconnect was a result of his actions which were saying, "You are a threat to my position and I am going to limit your exposure to upper management to protect myself." I went from someone who was highly motivated, who was delivering an exceptional performance that had brought me to the brink of a promotion, to someone with a deep loss of motivation that eventually resulted in me leaving the company. My decision to leave was not one that I think served me or the bank very well.

My supervisor wrongly determined that the answer to my diminished performance was to reiterate the expectations. This would be in line with traditional leadership principles—clearly expressing your expectations to your employees. Problem solved, right? What he was not taking into consideration was the effect his actions were having on my motivation. Your employees' motivation is more influenced by your actions than your words, especially if they contradict. Your actions will always set the precedent.

For example, if you only tell your employees what to do and never ask them what they think, you are in essence saying that they are not paid to think, you don't believe they can think, or you don't value what they think. An employee will rarely rise above the expectation you set by your actions, or in some cases, by your inaction. For the employee who is smart and driven, he may push through your limited expectation for a while and try to rise above it. If, however, he continues to get pushback when he shows initiative like thinking or identifying a problem, he will soon abandon the pursuit. Once the employee has reached that place, he is now under the lid of your expectation: *I am not paid to think or speak; there is no currency or value in these kind of actions.*

Remember that already motivated employees have a high sense of value even before they start a job, if for no other reason than just because they landed the job. I have met few people who were not excited about starting a new job, most likely because they are hoping it will be better than the one they are leaving. Emotions like excitement are a very important, significant ingredient in human motivation.

In the beginning of the movie *Hitch,* Will Smith, who plays Hitch, is giving relationship advice. The scene is shot during a cab ride, jumping between three men whom Hitch has helped to get noticed and get the first date with the lady of their dreams. As he is giving them instructions on how to have a successful first date, he says to them, "When you're wondering what to say or how you look, just remember, she's already out with you. That means she said yes when she could have said no. That means she made a plan when she could have just blown you off. So that means it's no longer your job to make her like you. It's your job not to mess it up." Leaders should keep in mind that their employees already said yes to the job. They are already emotionally invested, excited about the new opportunity. During the hiring process, we should have already qualified them as motivated, productive people. It is our job not to mess that up.

Feedback and Motivation

A hallmark of an exceptional company culture is the encouragement of feedback. We have talked about it before; nothing instills value like being asked what you think. It is such a simple thing and yet it can potentially raise workplace currency up off the charts. I am not talking about providing an open invitation to hate speech couched as criticism, though it is important to allow disagreement. I am talking about asking for someone's analysis and their evaluation of the process.

Employees are on the front lines, they are the ones executing the process. It stands to reason that they might just have an idea or two about how things should be done. Upper management can become so far removed from the front lines, they tend to lose touch with its reality. Yes, I just said that out loud.

In practical application, feedback is a simple transaction. My employees have the freedom to express their ideas and I have the freedom to accept or reject their suggestions. But I don't just blatantly disregard or discount an employee's idea and risk making them feel stupid. If I choose not to implement an employee's idea, it benefits the team to provide an explanation as to why I rejected it. If I make that effort, they know that though I may not implement every idea, I am still honestly interested in what they think and I give careful consideration to their ideas and opinions.

If your tendency is to repeatedly reject the ideas submitted by your employees, pounding them into the ground for daring to share them, then inviting feedback becomes nothing more than a platitude. By consistently rejecting solicited feedback, your actions are saying that feedback is not really welcome at all. A smart leader will always solicit input and listen to those who are executing the task and never discount what they say. Even the complaints can tell you about something that needs to change or needs attention; you just have to read between the lines.

Inviting feedback and implementing the ideas of your staff builds incredible trust between you and your employees if you execute the process with sincerity and transparency. A culture that encourages the fair exchange of ideas raises the bar of workplace currency across the entire organization. Research compiled by Dan Cable of the London Business School shows that those employees who feel welcome to express their "authentic" selves at work exhibit higher levels of organizational commitment, individual performance, and a propensity to help others (Goffee 2013). I interpret part of authentic to mean they are part of the conversation and have the freedom to express what they think.

There are those "no bad news" managers who refuse to hear anything that is not a positive report and have no tolerance for anything contrary to "success talk." Their philosophy is full speed ahead and to hell with everything else; we are unsinkable. I am pretty sure that's how things went on the *Titanic* (my proverbial go-to). Unfortunately, this kind of mindset always seems to lend itself to sinking the ship. Denying that there are real problems only means that you are not taking an honest look at your business and yourself. It is much easier just to attribute problems in business to ungrateful employees. Besides, that's a much easier fix, right? Maintaining a successful business requires an ongoing, honest evaluation of the business and the leaders who are running it, even when it raises some unpleasant issues. I have mentioned Howard Schultz before. This is one of his most noteworthy characteristics. As you read his story in *Onward*, it is the thing that immediately stands out to you.

In 1993, the company IBM was at a serious crossroads.

Having badly misread the rise of the personal computer and client-server computing, IBM suffered an $8 billion loss in 1993. This was the third straight year the company had suffered a billion-dollar loss. The problem was that management at the time was stubbornly refusing to change their current culture. Finally, whether due to the persistent losses in profit or other reasons, they had a moment of self-evaluation resulting in a very unusual decision for IBM. For the first time since its founding, IBM brought in an outsider to take the helm. Louis V. Gerstner, Jr., formerly of RJR Nabisco and American Express, became CEO of Big Blue.

Gerstner brought with him a new way of thinking. His first order of business was to begin listening to frontline employees and their clients. He found that the clients needed expert assistance to help them integrate all the separate computer technologies that were emerging at the time. Who better to fill that role than a company with a global reach in a wide variety of areas? Gerstner also realized there had to be a radical shift in the way managers at IBM managed their people. The focus needed to change from the command and control type management that so dominated their culture, to creating a more participative culture where employees were enabled to perform their jobs better, smarter, and more effectively. This meant shifting the culture where previously the conversation was limited to management to a broader dialogue that involved employees, creating a more collaborative environment. This would help more readily identify necessary changes to put IBM on back on track.

The result: By 1994, IBM returned to profitability, earning profits of $3 billion and lived to celebrate their 100th birthday as a company back in 2011. To their credit, very few corporations survive for that many years. They celebrated their centennial with record sales, record profits, and a record share price. As to their future, Gerstner stepped down in 2011 and passed the baton to CEO Virginia Rometty in 2012. Under fire in 2014 for another Big Blue crisis, the new CEO, being questioned by a group of New York analysts, simply said, "Look, this is not the first time we've transformed; this will not be the last time" (Summer 2014). When a company is willing to take an honest look at their culture, like IBM did, the chances of survival increase significantly.

Emotion and Motivation

In *Conscious Capitalism*, Mackey and Sisodia define how people feel about their work and how it impacts their motivation.

Work is just a job: Our job is a transaction where we trade a certain number of hours per week for a paycheck with no emotional connection to it.

Work is a career: Ambitious-minded people see work only as an opportunity to climb the corporate ladder to attain the rewards that go with it. This approach can still be empty of emotional connection and the investment made is only motivated by money. They point out that this kind of motivation can be based on self-serving interests, which can be damaging to their co-workers and ultimately, the company.

Work is a calling: When we see our work as a calling, we gain value and satisfaction beyond the financial rewards. Work can be something we are passionate about, something that makes us feel that we are making a difference in the world. The authors' claim is that this view lends itself to the employee feeling more engaged, more alive and motivated to stay with the job longer.

We could easily define engagement as the emotional investment a person has in a thing or endeavor. As leaders, we cannot underestimate how people "feel" about their jobs and how our words and actions impact the way they view their job. How emotionally invested a person is naturally carries over into their motivation. Workplace currency is significant because of its impact on emotional investment and therefore, on a person's motivation. Take any part of employee behavior behind the work culture and break it down; it is always about currency.

The Currency of Culture
Because the core values that make up a culture, regardless of whether they are defined or undefined, influence things like motivation, innovation and overall performance, culture is the currency of your company. We must recognize culture's currency, its value and its impact on the success of a company. When a company is at a point of crisis, the resolution almost always necessitates a change in culture. If our sole purpose for existence is only the pursuit of profits, we will strangle our own culture in the process. On the other hand, if we put our efforts into creating an exceptional and engaging culture, defining it by the right core values, rise in profits will follow, as proven by companies like Whole Foods, Starbucks, Google and others. Culture is the true currency.

But we're not quite done yet. ∎

CHAPTER NINE

Trust

Transparency Required

"When people honor each other, there is a trust established that leads to synergy, interdependence, and deep respect. Both parties make decisions and choices based on what is right, what is best, what is valued most highly."

—Blaine Lee

Edelman is a public relations firm that conducts an annual global study to explore corporate trust issues. Their 2013 Edelman Trust Barometer was the largest survey of its kind, including more than 31,000 respondents from 26 markets around the world. What that survey revealed is that there is a deep distrust of leadership within organizations. But that's not a news flash to anyone, is it? Leaders are perceived as looking out for their own interest at the expense of the interests of others. Leaders are perceived as dictating—not leading—through fear and intimidation. No one crosses these leaders because of a fear of repercussions either though job loss or a ruined career. These leaders seem to be accountable to no one because they have all the power. Usually, it takes some monumental event where the control-hungry leader colors too far outside the lines, usually doing something questionable or unethical, for the leader to be forced from their position by another entity who has to come in and rectify the problem. All of this has brought us to a serious place of disconnect where few trust their leaders.

Culture of Suspicion

Trust does not seem to carry the value it once did but it has tremendous impact on how people feel about their job and about those for whom they work, both of which impact performance. It is unacceptable to simply resign to live without it.

I can remember managing five contractors who were all interested in becoming full-time employees of the company for which I worked. One morning, the president of the company sent a revised organization chart to everyone's email. This was a younger company and at that time, a thing like an organization chart was a work in progress. Only one of the five contractors was listed on the chart. The other four, upon seeing the chart, assumed this contractor had been hired full time. As you might have guessed the chart created a great disturbance, even bringing one of the other contractors to tears. When I first saw the chart, I initially didn't think anything about the omission of the other four contractors because there were other inaccuracies on the chart as well and I didn't even know whether they were included on the email distribution list. I happened to be out of the office that day for a time after the email came out and missed all the drama that occurred over the chart, but I heard about it when I came back. Fortunately, my manager took care of clarifying the inaccuracies of the chart for everyone involved.

I tell this story because I think it illustrates the underlying suspicions that many times exist in a corporate culture.

My contactor group just assumed their fellow contractor was hired and no one else was considered. I had seen that scenario play out so many times in my work experience that I probably would have made the same assumption. Once I returned to the office, I acknowledged what had happened and sent this simple message: "I heard about the confusion today over the organization chart. Let me assure you, I would not hire someone without informing the rest of the group not only of the decision, but also why I made the decision to hire that specific person."

I would not say it is often a chief characteristic of management to be that truthful. Maybe like Jack Nicholson's character in *A Few Good Men,* perhaps we assume our employees can't handle the truth. I will say that managers are not often obligated to be that truthful with their employees. In some scenarios, managers are given very little wiggle room concerning what they can and cannot say because of the liability issues in today's marketplace. However, communicating as much as possible within the given parameters goes a long way toward disarming suspicion and developing trust. If you are intent on creating an exceptional culture in which extraordinary performance can take place, the establishment of trust must be high on your list. You cannot have a successful collaborative culture without it. I saw an immediate change in my group of contractors shortly after I sent my email. The trust level had been raised a few notches.

One of the chief characteristics of Herb Kelleher, founder and former CEO of Southwest Airlines, was his upfront and straightforward leadership style. This built credibility with the employees at Southwest because of his long and consistent history of transparency and honesty. In addition, he made himself accessible and approachable to Southwest employees, always available to find ways to help people out. The company had a no-layoff record under Kelleher, upheld even in the downturns of business. Under Kelleher's replacement, Gary Kelly, that same policy has been upheld. Kelly strives to be a collaborative leader and encourages open communication and teamwork. These are the characteristics of leadership that build trust. Some leaders you only see when there is a problem.

Too often, the resident of the corner office is viewed with suspicion; as a hindrance instead of a help to their employees. If you discover your employees addressing you as "your hindership" you might want to take that seriously. A lack of trust all but ensures the impossibility of building any kind of healthy work culture. If there is no trust, neither the leader nor the employee has any measure of workplace currency. It is a bankrupt culture. Yes, currency is a two-way street.

Having a culture of suspicion makes it difficult for people to perform their job at even the most basic of levels, much less deliver any kind of extraordinary performance. Studies in human nature may suggest that we are naturally suspicious, but that is not the prevailing attitude you want in your company's culture. Suspicion cultivates a culture based in fear. Suspicion will quickly undermine any possibility of a collaborative effort and will have a detrimental impact on the success of any endeavor. Don't let it go unchecked!

Micromanagement

Allow me to get in the weeds here a bit. Micromanagement is based in perfectionism. Perfectionism is approval based, in that the inward driver is the fear one has of the loss of approval if they don't measure up. In a real sense, perfectionists don't just micromanage others, they micromanage themselves. As employees, perfectionists are loved because they produce a high quality of work. In most cases they can be very driven, even if it is out of the unhealthy motivation of fear. The more extreme will work eighty hours a week if needed to make sure they get it all done and get it all right to satisfy the internal voice that drives them. For their efforts, they will be highly praised and highly rewarded and in some cases, work themselves to an early grave as we continue to applaud them. It would seem right to promote them to manage other people. But once promoted, their approval is tied to the performance of others. The opportunity to lose approval is also now amplified by others. The only way to ensure there is no loss of approval is to micromanage every detail. There are a couple of ways micromanagers try to get this done. The most obvious is the fear-based management style. Since their internal driver is fear, it only stands to reason that fear would be their "go-to" as they manage others. Their reasoning is that if people are afraid to mess up, then there will be fewer mistakes. The other way is to limit the tasks that the employees are assigned, therefore limiting the chance of them messing something up.

Micromanagers are typically poor delegators. This means they are usually overloaded, which can lead to feelings of resentment as they feel they have to do it all. Employees, in return, resent this type of fear-based management style and so appreciation is not forthcoming, which furthers the feelings of resentment the micromanager already has. It is a self-perpetuating dilemma.

An employee who is micromanaged is negatively affected by the presence of someone always looking over their shoulder. Usually, a very nervous someone. Because of the lack of delegation, employees are rarely challenged by anything new and so their development opportunities are very limited. The combination of all these things makes for a very stressful, volatile working relationship simply because this kind of manager has difficulty trusting others to get the work done and done right.

I have yet to meet anyone who loves being micromanaged.

It is contrary to human nature. It is an infringement on autonomy. It's the equivalent of being treated like a child. Much of micromanagement is deeply rooted in a desire to control, in fear, and insecurity—hardly the building blocks for a culture of trust. Micromanagers are very difficult to work for, and yet I'd venture to say we have all worked for a micromanager at one time or another. You never really measure up for this kind of leader. Nine times out of ten, they will set you up to fail without even realizing it. But even if they do realize it, don't expect to them to accept responsibility. Since much of micromanagement is rooted in insecurity, these kinds of leaders are incapable of acknowledging when they are at fault. Somehow they think that accepting responsibility for their errors makes them look weak. In an effort to maintain their own currency, they undermine the currency of those who work for them. They can appear to be self-serving but in truth, they are just afraid.

A better model of management is trust with accountability; it is a better and more effective methodology. People don't resent being asked to report their production, as long as they have confidence that their report will be judged fairly and equitably. But no one likes being under someone else's thumb, usually with the screws being put to them. Build a management style based on trust and you will grow exceptional, loyal, and productive people. You will have built your house upon the rock. Build on distrust and it will choke the life out of your people and your organization. You will have built your house on the sand.

Controlling Leaders

In extreme cases where there is paranoia and a measure of personality disorder, when conflict arises, a controlling manager can become irrational and it is difficult, if not impossible, to resolve real problems. Most certainly, the employee will always be viewed as the source of the problem by this kind of manager. He will either victimize his employee, usually in an effort to demoralize, or he may childishly take on the role of the victim himself, which prohibits any mature, adult resolution to the issue at hand. Since the real problem is never addressed, the conflict continues to resurface and the working relationship spirals downward until somebody has to leave—usually the one who has the least amount of control. The result is a culture rife with negative stress, fear and ultimately, uncertainty. People are walking on eggshells and they are most certainly glad when the boss is out of the office for the day. This is just another example of disconnect; a kind of disconnect that is fueled by uncertainty. Uncertainty causes people to pull back and disengage. They are also less likely to fully invest in something when they are unsure of its future. If you doubt this statement on human nature, just watch the stock market.

Suspicion

As I have said before, disconnect is the enemy; connection is your friend. Because so much of disconnect is often rooted in suspicion, it is important we make a determination to guard against it. Suspicion germinates in the presupposition that people will fail you. In your suspicion, you act in such a way as to set others up to fail while setting yourself up to be proven right. If you hold to this mindset, people will inevitably disappoint you because that is what you expected from the start. It is not that they are fulfilling your expectation, but more that your suspicion created a reality in which they were forced to live. You believed the lie that people will always fail you and in so believing, you inadvertently brought it to pass. Suspicion colors everything that is said and done.

Suspicion will always lead you to flawed conclusions. You so strongly believe a thing to be true that you will accept lies and false accusations if they support your flawed conclusions. There will be no defense your people can offer that will change your mind. This leaves both you and your employees trapped in your lie. If suspicion is allowed to go unchecked, you will continually repeat the process over and over again, thinking the problem is with "all those people out there" when the one constant in all of it is you.

Leaders who do not trust, can themselves not be trusted. That is a hard statement, I know, but trust and suspicion cannot co-exist. You have to choose whether you will take the easier path—suspicion—or follow the more difficult path to trust. Cultivating trust will require a deliberate choice and determined effort. But it is an essential dynamic to building an exceptional and engaging culture.

Trust Breeds Trust
On the more positive side of this issue, we see that trust breeds trust. It is impossible to build an exceptional and engaging culture without trust. People are much more productive when they work within a culture of trust. Fear can drive production, but only to certain levels and only for a certain amount of time. Fear will eventually drain the energy out of your people and burn them out, at which point production will decline. The gains generated by fear are short lived as uncertainty and insecurity lead to disconnect. However, things like innovation and creativity—components of exceptional performance—will be cultivated in an atmosphere where people feel a sense of certainty and security founded on trust.

Trust is the glue that holds a team together. If you embrace the body model of organization (my recommendation, because it works) then your goal is for your business to operate in a fluid, forward motion with all the parts of your company working together toward a common end. Your physical body cannot have the different parts opposing each other, going in opposite directions. If that were the case, you wouldn't even be able to perform basic functions like walking because of the disorder created by the lack of unity. Unity requires trust.

To operate efficiently, a company must have a unified direction. Unified direction requires creating and maintaining a culture of trust. Distrust creates disunity. People will disconnect from what they cannot trust for the sake of self-preservation. The presence of trust in an organization, however, means real problems can get resolved; people communicate and collaborate without fear and unified forward movement can be achieved. Without trust, you have a culture that will continually perpetuate disconnect. But if I can trust what you say and I can trust you with what I say without the fear of retaliation, we can create a successful collaborative culture.

Trust and Communication

Trust is the channel through which good communication flows. Trust grows when people speak the truth, hedging nothing, and when they show respect for the diverse ideas and perspectives presented. The worst kind of leader has no regard for confidentiality and no concept of discretion. He takes things that people say to him and either uses those words against them at an opportune time or uses those words to discredit them with other people. This type of leader will add a spin on things to make the comments more venomous. It's a terrible thing not to be able to trust what someone says and worse, to not be able to trust them with what you say.

I'm not advocating that you manage with blind trust. I have always told my children that trust is their most valuable commodity. Trust brings freedom, promotion and money. When my kids were in their formative teenage years, they thought trust should be given out blindly, no questions asked. As they matured, they came to understand that trust is actually extended based on information they provided—where you are going, what you are doing, who you are going to do it with, call if something changes—you get the picture. As long as that information was forthcoming, trust was extended. In return, I had to demonstrate that I could be trusted with what they told me.

Transparency

Trust requires accountability from leaders. A smart leader knows that transparency is essential to accountability. If anything is missing in leadership in our current society, it is transparency. Of course for a leader to be transparent, that would require they tell the truth. A novel idea, I know. When my two-year-old granddaughter does something suspect, her first inclination is to hide or cover up the behavior. This is a true testimony to human nature.

If a leader would make himself accountable to those he serves, there would be no need for extreme measures to get him back into line when he goes out of control. Then again, if he makes himself accountable, chances are he won't go out of control in the first place. We have done our leaders no favors by allowing them to proceed without accountability. The history of human nature does not speak well to one man's ability to handle unchecked power.

We can all become easily enamored by our own success. The business term for this phenomenon is hubris and research tells us when we reach this state of *hubris,* we begin our descent. Smart leaders avoid hubris through accountability, transparency and personal evaluation. This also makes them inherently trustworthy in the eyes of those who work for them.

Smart leaders are transparent. For the most obvious reason, it builds trust. In 2008, then-senator Barack Obama set transparency as one of the foundational tenants of his presidential campaign. President Barack Obama still claims his presidency has been marked by a high level of transparency, despite the endless barrage of scandals and suspected cover-ups and other contradictory behavior. His drop in approval ratings in 2014 may tell a different story.

Granted, transparency is no cakewalk, but the lack of transparency can bite you in the end (butt). Just ask Tony Hayward, former CEO of British Petroleum. On April 20, 2010, fifty miles off the coast of Louisiana, there was an explosion on the Deepwater Horizon oil rig in the Gulf of Mexico. Eleven lives were lost in the explosion and it became the worst ecosystem disaster of the Gulf Coast in history.

On May 11, 2010, three executives were brought before a Senate Committee: Lamar McKay, BP America president, Steven Newman, Transocean president, and Tim Probert, Halliburton Global Business president. Ironically, President Obama (early in his presidency) would call their finger pointing a "ridiculous spectacle" as each blamed the event on the other's company. Forty-three days after the explosion, BP's stock had plummeted 40% (Webley 2010). (As of this writing, four years after the spill, BP's stock has still not fully recovered.) Fifty-nine days after the explosion, the well was still spewing crude into the Gulf. Multiple attempts to cap the well had failed. Pictures of oil-covered wildlife were all over the television.

On June 17, 2010, Tony Hayward was brought before a U.S. House Committee but in the same fashion as the other executives, rather than assume responsibility for what happened, he attempted to spin the situation away from BP. His angle: there were too many different companies involved to know who was really responsible. *Time* magazine listed a few of his responses from that day:

- I can't possibly know why the decisions were made (on the rig).
- I don't know.

- I can't answer because I wasn't there.
- I am afraid I can't recall.
- That was a decision I was not party to (Walsh 2010).

Many times, leaders like Hayward attempt to manage problems by minimizing them or shifting the blame, attempting to lead the public to believe it's not as bad as it looks or it wasn't their fault. Playing the blame game goes all the way back to the beginning of time in the garden. Adam blamed Eve and Eve blamed the snake for why she ate from the forbidden tree. We all tend to want to hide our sin. In the case of the BP spill, I am sure there were pressures coming from all sides to "handle" the situation and a call for damage control, whether from a board or investors or others. In reality, these are business culture issues that undermine trust and impede transparency. It is unlikely that those culture issues just suddenly appeared simultaneously with the spill. For Tony Hayward, the end result was his resignation as CEO from BP, mostly brought on by how he handled the situation, which drew so much negative press it would be more difficult for BP to recover their image if he remained at the helm. In the end, transparency would most likely have played better than the dodge the bullet strategy that was used. Nirmalya Kumar, professor of marketing at London Business School, says BP missed on all four crisis management tools: candor, compassion, commitment and contrition (Walt 2010). I would identify those as the four characteristics of transparency.

Outside of the 11 lives lost, the attempt at damage control proved to be more costly to BP's image and in the larger picture, hurt the overall image of the oil and gas industry. Smart leaders understand the value of transparency and its impact on building a culture of trust within and without. As leaders, we must make sure our commitment to transparency goes beyond just a verbal accolade and is instead a value that is demonstrated on a consistent basis. It is, without a doubt, the road less traveled.

Trust: A Building Block of Collaboration

I have mentioned before how people withhold information to maintain their own position within an organization and how I have been deliberately left out of meetings in order to minimize my exposure to upper management and jeopardize my future with the company. Those who would do such things are the kind of people who undermine trust and the collaborative effort of the group. Even if such behavior is fear based, the bottom line is those who exhibit such behavior are only looking out for themselves. They cannot be trusted.

Distrust is how competition becomes an unhealthy force in your organization, rather than the positive force it should be to encourage your people to reach higher professional levels. Unhealthy competition rooted in distrust has as its goal the elimination of others who are perceived as standing in the way. If people feel they must undermine others in order to advance themselves or at least maintain their own position and status, how can you expect to build trust in that environment?

One of the greatest ways to build trust is to solve problems together. After all, collaboration is nothing more than a collection of diverse individuals forged together through trust using communication and teamwork to pursue a common purpose. Solving problems together helps those you lead learn what is inside of you as you learn what is inside them. Trust is difficult to establish if you are never afforded a real look at what is inside another. Your team needs to see that you're a real person and a "for-real" person. This is so valuable in building an engaging culture within your team. If I took a poll of your direct reports and asked them the simple question "Is your boss a real person," their answers would tell me a lot about the effectiveness of your leadership.

I didn't include trust as a fundamental element of collaboration back in chapter four because of its influence on everything we do. The presence of trust undergirds and lifts everything we do to much higher levels. We cannot underestimate its importance in creating an exceptional culture. Since fear and trust cannot co-exist, we must have a culture that is open, accepting and honest, even when we get something wrong. Trust; transparency required! ▪

CHAPTER TEN

Motivating Millennials
They Want to Change the World

"Purpose inspires people. Purpose releases creativity."
—John Mackey

I t's not hard to figure out millennials. They want to change the world. Why? Because someone told them they could. In an interview with *E!,* Selena Gomez, when asked about dating, made this statement: "I do think I might scare some guys, because I'm like, 'I want to change the world! I have dreams! What do *you* want to do?'" Though the question was asked in reference to dating, her answer is a good example of how millennials think. They translate their accomplishments into what John Mackey calls a "higher purpose," defined as the difference you want to make in the world (Mackey 2014). Intrinsic to their motivation, they want to change the world in some meaningful way. Many of their influences such as teachers, pastors and mentors called them world changers. I have six millennial children of my own and yes, I told them it is possible to change the world.

Millennials are most often defined as the generation born between the early 1980s and the early 2000s, currently aged 15 to 35. Estimates say millennials make up somewhere around 36% of the current workforce and that number is expected to rise to as much as 50% by as early as 2015. Sources all agree that by 2025, millennials will make up 75% of the workforce.

To understand millennials is to understand their parents. They were raised by baby boomers, so most likely they heard all the complaints about the injustices of the old corporate business hierarchies. You might think millennials dislike authority for this reason, but it is not a blatant rejection of authority. Most have moderately healthy relationships with adults. Their assumed rejection of authority is more of a rejection of old, worn-out practices. It is the nature and philosophy behind the hierarchies that generally do not interest them, and millennials don't get behind ideas they don't believe in. Sometimes that comes across as a rejection of authority. They typically reject practices that are inequitable, bias ridden and as I mentioned before, systems that are unjust that their parents lived with. These are the kinds of things they want to change in the world.

I do not think it is coincidental that there is currently so much emphasis on company culture. The parents of these millennials put a great deal of value on family. Family was about creating a culture, a culture that was characterized by trust, communication, personal growth and development, finding your purpose and working together to achieve a common goal. While much of American business led by baby boomers has bottom line profits as the primary driving force, their children value company culture much more highly and they are looking for a culture that possesses the same kind of core values that were present in their home.

Parents of millennials wanted to have a meaningful relationship with their children, perhaps because such a relationship was missing in their own upbringing. Ironically, even though the parents put emphasis on relationship, they were typically more accepting of environments where there were relationship voids. In contrast, their millennial children think this is the normal way to relate to adults—through relationship—therefore, they have a different set of expectations. If you not believe that building relationships is the basis for working together, then by their standards, you simply are not getting it right. This has resulted in millennials having a more flat view of the world in terms of how they relate to people.

Millennials respond to leaders who are relational. They will respect your authority and give you their loyalty if they feel you value relationship. Otherwise they won't waste their time with you, because you can't give them what they want. The expectation is that within relationship they are allowed to be heard, to express their opinion, to express their ideas. Relationship says I matter, I am valued and since I matter, you are most likely to help me in my pursuits. Translated, that means you will provide me with opportunities for growth and development to reach my full potential.

For a millennial, relationship is all about trust. They will not follow you unless they trust you and before they can trust you, you must first establish a relationship with them. Trust is formed as those in leadership take the time to relate to their subordinates, showing a genuine interest in who they are and interacting with them on a personal level. If you will listen to the opinions of millennials and show that you value their opinions, they will trust you. If they feel valued and feel they can trust you, they are more than willing to invest in the organization. Close to the idea of trust is transparency. You don't have to be perfect, but they want you to be upfront, above board and honest about your shortcomings. If they know that you are genuinely interested in their development and their pursuits outside of your own agenda, they will typically put up with any of your less-than-desirable qualities. I know of an up and coming business, Thrive15, where the majority of employees are millennials; in fact, some of my children work there. Sometimes the owner can be tough to work for in that he expects a lot of his people, but one thing my children know is this man is genuinely interested in their dreams and in helping them achieve those dreams.

My wife recently talked with a young lady who is a well-educated millennial working for a very prestigious company within the same industry in which she works. To my surprise, after the conversation she sent an email to my wife indicating that because of the lack of development opportunities within her company, she was looking for employment elsewhere. Development is a big key to their internal motivators.

It is no secret that most millennials are best motivated through affirmation. Sure, everyone likes to be stroked, but millennials seem to develop better through affirmation. This is not to say you can't be truthful with them about their performance, but as I said earlier, they have to know you are interested in their development, their future and their forward movement. If you are the type of leader who feels like this younger generation needs to be put in their place, you will one day soon find that no one from this millennial generation is following you. And if the stats are true, that means 50 to 75% of the future workforce won't have anything to do with you. If you're the type of leader who degrades people, thinking that fear and humiliation is good for motivation, you will find yourself with a very high turnover rate. Think of it like magnets, when they are aligned the right way they attract; misaligned, they repel. Millennials simply won't continually commit time to anything that looks or sounds like negative energy. However, even if you're a demanding manager, if they feel at the end of the day they are better equipped for their future, they will stick around. Again, it is about forward movement and personal growth for this group, affirmation being a big key to what motivates them.

Millennials are actually very forgiving and in some ways, more tolerant than their baby boomers parents. They are not looking for perfection; they know Jesus walked on water and that you are not Him. Be willing to admit when you are wrong and give them credit when they are right. They expect you to give them credit for their own ideas—novel idea, I know. I can remember one millennial talking to another who was new on the job, explaining that their boss didn't accept ideas that were not his own. Yes, there are people like that out there; maybe you have met a few. He told his new co-worker that in fact, if you had an idea on how to do something better, you had to make this manager think it was his idea for him to use it. Maybe that was his way of giving his manager affirmation, sort of sharing the love. This was very insightful on the part of the veteran millennial, but the travesty is that this manager was so dysfunctional in his thinking in the first place. These two millennials were both more tolerant than I would have been but over time, I bet they would become less so. Then again, maybe they just viewed that manager as an antique and were counting on him being gone soon or they were planning on not staying long.

Millennials have been taught to be creative and innovative by their parents, so they generally have a head full of good ideas. I can remember my wife in our early parenting years reading about how to raise creative children. Instead of giving them coloring books with pictures to color, they were given plain paper with crayons. This was supposed to encourage free expression and to stimulate imagination. Of course for the sake of encouragement, in my wife's eyes, that meant every paper was a work of art. It's not that they were just coloring outside the lines; they had no lines. This explains why millennials tend to be highly motivated in the free and unhindered art of creative and innovative expression. They are innovators, if you haven't noticed, and that's a good thing because their world demands it. This creative energy gives them the competitive edge in today's job market.

This is the area, however, where they can butt heads with the hierarchal systems that limit creative intelligence to just a few. They refuse to be left out of the conversation. But those companies who develop a culture where millennials can engage their creative intelligence will have found themselves a gold mine. Google is a good example of this type of company in that the organization structure is flat and every employee is given the opportunity to express ideas to the whole of their internal business community. Employees are also allowed to use 20% of their time at work to pursue projects that interest them. Do we even need to discuss the success of Google? What they're doing works.

The reason millennials want credit for their ideas is because that is how they feel connected to the business. They have little tolerance for a manager who is unwilling to accept them on those terms. They are looking for workplace currency, seeing it as part of their validation. Remember, millennials want to change the world and they want to do it today through the expression of their own innovative ideas.

Remember, to completely understand the motivations of millennials, you have to understand the motivations of their parents. They did not want their kids to be hindered or stifled in any way. They wanted them to reach their full potential; this was basic to their parenting style. There was no "children should be seen and not heard" in their mindset.

I remember when my son was about five, we participated in a ministry to the poor through our church. I took my oldest son with me, that relationship thing, as I went to serve. When we came home, my son asked me if he could go look for some poor people in our neighborhood. Since we had just come back from working at a ministry to the poor, I wasn't going to squelch such an inclination, so I told him yes he could, with the simple instruction for him to stay on our street. He was gone for a short time and then he came back to the house.

Later we learned from a neighbor that he had come to their door and when they answered his knock, he asked them if there were any poor people in their house. This was a middle-class neighborhood, which was one of the reasons I let my son go off on his own as I knew the likelihood of his finding a poor person was slim. My wife was horrified at that thought that her child had gone to the door and asked such a question, as most mothers might be, but before she had a chance to express her displeasure, I stopped her. Our son had demonstrated such an undaunted boldness and fearlessness that day at the young age of five, I wasn't going to risk stifling something that as an adult, he was going to need. I knew those personality traits would serve him well someday when he was grown and making his way in this world. If you met my son today, I think you would agree it paid off.

Millennials seem to have little tolerance for stupid. They are smart, having been raised by smart parents who made sure their children benefited from their own experience. If they asked their parents "why" about something, they typically were not told, "Because I said so." Their parents took the time to provide the rationale behind the decisions, creating a life-lesson moment.

Along these same lines, millennials were allowed to express their opinions within the family culture, to have a voice. This is not to say they always got their way. It just means they view authority differently. Don't expect them to automatically respect you because they should. They will respect you because you took the time to have an intelligent conversation with them and didn't treat them as if they were simply under-lings. If there is a problem, they expect you to give them the chance to tell their side of the story. If you offer them some-thing they value, they can be highly appreciative when you deliver and they will gladly reciprocate the gesture, giving back to you their hard work and loyalty. They will appreciate your experience and wisdom but don't expect them to bow, kiss the ring on your finger and worship the ground you walk on (okay, so I am exaggerating to make a point). They will view your experience as something that will get them where they want to go faster. They will think it is a fair exchange for their hard work.

Millennials are great collaborators. Remember, they were raised in families where everyone worked together to achieve a common goal, yet they were given individual recognition for their part. This is not to say they are not competitive, but the better ones will make room for other people, wanting to see everyone succeed. Perhaps you thought it a bad idea that everyone received a trophy in those Little League days, but it taught millennials the value of a team and that everyone can enjoy the rewards of a team effort when everyone works hard toward the common objective.

It is important to millennials that they are a part of and feel connected to something bigger than themselves. That requires that you present a clear objective and support that objective with a set of core values. And yes, they expect you to live those values in front of them. I know, so many novel ideas from one generation.

It is not enough for them to sit behind a desk for eight hours a day, working blindly. They want to see the bigger pic-ture so as to understand why they are doing something. The "why" is a big deal for them because the meaning of their task is found in the "why." This brings us back to that whole "change the world" thing. It is not enough to know and recite the vision of the company; they must "feel" connected to it and to the core values of the culture, both in their head and their heart. Blame it on *Star Wars* if you will, but nonetheless how Master Yoda thinks has somehow found its way into their thinking:

> *"For my ally is the Force—and a powerful ally it is. Life creates it, makes it grow. Its energy surrounds us and binds us. Luminous beings are we, not this crude matter. You must feel the Force around you: here, between you, me, the tree, the rock, everywhere, yes, even between the land and the ship."*
> —Star Wars Episode V: The Empire Strikes Back

Yes, this episode was released before most of them were born, but their parents made sure they watched it on video. Companies are realizing they need to attract this unique group of people called millennials and having them in the mix is benefitting everyone in the organization. For instance, millennials typically want more flexibility at work. They want to pursue outside interests. As a result, companies are offering flexible hours and programs such as the 9/80 schedule in which employees have every other Friday off by working four nine-hour days each week. Millennials love this, but many of the older company veterans are taking advantage of this same schedule.

There are a number of other ways companies are adopting and creating cultures compatible with this generation. For instance, XTO Energy states on their website under the "Company Culture" section, "At XTO Energy, we promote an entrepreneurial spirit and perspective. We are always looking for experienced individuals who take a fresh look at the job. We engage a management style that promotes the free exchange of new ideas and rewards self-motivation. As such, we rely on our people who are driven to do their jobs well, working as if the company were their very own."

A more familiar company, Starbucks, is also a good example. We cited their mission statement earlier, but for context, let me restate it: "Our mission: to inspire and nurture the human spirit—one person, one cup and one neighborhood at a time." The focus of this mission extends to their employees, whom they call "partners." This is what they say: "Our Partners: We're called partners, because it's not just a job, it's our passion. Together, we embrace diversity to create a place where each of us can be ourselves. We always treat each other with respect and dignity. And we hold each other to that standard."

Notice the use of "partners" instead of employees, the use of "our passion" instead of it just being a job, embracing "diversity," creating a culture where people can be who they are, treated with dignity and respect. These are the kinds of ideas that attract millennials.

Google, which was mentioned earlier in this chapter, says this about their company culture: "We strive to maintain the open culture often associated with start-ups, in which everyone is a hands-on contributor and feels comfortable sharing ideas and opinions. In our weekly all-hands ("TGIF") meetings—not to mention over email or in the cafe—Googlers ask questions directly to Larry, Sergey and other execs about any number of company issues. Our offices and cafes are designed to encourage interactions between Googlers within and across teams, and to spark conversation about work as well as play."

I am of the opinion that this generation is already migrating toward companies that hold to many of these ideas. Another example of a company that espouses these same types of ideas is Whole Foods, as described in Mackey's *Conscious Capitalism*. You may not have to adopt all these ideas, but you will need to hit on at least a few to attract this crowd. One of the main ideas is a company must have what the author calls a "Higher Purpose." When considering your company's higher purpose, you ask the questions, "Why do we exist and what contribution do we want to make in the world?" A higher purpose serves as inspiration for the workforce and raises the levels of creativity, collaboration, diligence, loyalty and passion (Mackey 2014).

Whether it is Mackey's intent to appeal directly to millennials, his ideas line up with many of the things we have talked about not only in this chapter but with the ideas inherent to the premise of the book; the importance of having an exceptional and engaging culture. Mackey states that culture must be characterized by values such as trust, accountability, transparency, loyalty, personal growth and others. The management style of such a company is based on decentralization, empowerment and collaboration.

If you are outside the millennial generation, you may have had the thought while reading this chapter that millennials are not unique; they are just like the rest of us. We all want to give our lives to something bigger than ourselves. We want our work to be meaningful, fulfilling and filled with purpose. We desire and value the same things in our work culture. The only real difference is that millennials will not settle for anything less, and companies are taking notice because they need to attract that talent. Sometimes it takes a generation to make a needed correction in the previous generation and move things in the right direction. We raised them to be who they are with the attitude "I will not be denied." We didn't sugar coat the facts of what it would take to make their ideals become a reality, we just told them it was possible. Millennials understand the currency of culture, which certainly will make corporate America a better place for us all. ∎

CHAPTER ELEVEN

Work/Life Balance
The Myths

"There are companies that focus on work-life separation or work-life balance and at Zappos, we really focus on work-life integration and at the end of the day it's just life ... and especially if you spend so much time at work, you better enjoy the time that you're spending there and people that you're with."
—Tony Hsieh

"The great enemy of the truth is very often not the lie, deliberate, contrived and dishonest, but the myth, persistent, persuasive and unrealistic."
—John F. Kennedy

I think the above Tony Hsieh quote is noteworthy. Considering the amount of time in our life that we spend at work, it should be time that brings a measure of fulfillment and satisfaction. Our work culture should provide the opportunity for employees to be happy in their jobs, instead of a being a place they experience negative stress and frustration. John Mackey contends that a fun workplace is a key to creating a culture that is both dynamic and innovative (Mackey 2014).

The term "work/life balance" is getting new attention, but what does it mean? An individual's view of it all depends on their hierarchy of values. For my wife and me, family has always been one of our primary values, which is why we had six kids. With having six kids, it really made no sense for my wife to work when the kids were little, as nearly all of her check would have gone to pay childcare expenses. But as our kids started school, the need for my wife to stay home lessened and she was able to return to the workforce. Those early years living on one income were pretty lean and we had our share of struggles, but now my wife and I are seeing more success in our careers. But we still put a high premium on family and for us, work/life balance means balancing our passion for family with our passion for the work we are doing.

For some, work is everything; it is at the top of their value hierarchy. They might even say, "I am doing it all for my family." With the expenses of raising a family and the cost of a college education, I can't deny there could be some justification for that kind of thinking. But then the issue becomes, is it ever enough? What if success takes longer to achieve than you anticipated or the price you're paying for working long hours is higher than you thought? The end result could be it will cost you your family.

There is more to consider to work/life balance than just putting value on family or hobbies or passions. Good work/life balance means putting value on your health, as well. In his book *The One Thing*, Gary Keller, co-founder of Keller Williams Realty, talks about his pursuit of success and describes it in this way: "For many years I suffered from trying to live the lies of success." Keller very intensely projected himself as the successful person he wanted to be through talk, walk and dress but for him, it was all a lie. Ironically his approach actually worked for a time, but eventually landed him in the hospital. He described himself in this way: "I bought into getting up before the crack of dawn, getting revved up playing inspirational theme songs, and getting going before anyone else." He was one of those bosses who would schedule meetings at 7:30 am and lock the door at 7:31, shutting out those who dared show up late. He believed this was the way to personal success and the way to push others to success as well. Keller claims, "This approach always worked, but in the end it pushed me too hard, others too far, and my world over the edge" (Keller 2012).

As I was writing the manuscript for this book, another book, *Thrive: The Third Metric to Redefining Success and Creating a Life of Well-Being, Wisdom, and Wonder* by Arianna Huffington came out and quickly became a *New York Times* best seller. As Huffington's title would indicate, success is being redefined. That book takes a closer look at the effect of working such long hours, as the author herself collapsed from exhaustion brought on by her overworked lifestyle in pursuit of success. It caused her to reevaluate and reassess the real value of all those hours in light of their associated cost.

Tim Ferriss' *The 4 Hour Workweek* became a *New York Times* best seller in five days. Whether or not the premise of the book is based in the issue of work/life balance, the short amount of time it took to get to the best seller list would indicate the topic of working less is something people are very interested in. Even when work is enjoyable, most people need an opportunity to unplug in a healthy way and to pursue other passions. Couple this with a demand created by the up and coming workforce called millennials, and what we're finding is companies are looking for ways to create schedules for their employees that allow for such opportunities.

In some companies, taking vacation is viewed as a sign

of weakness. While taking vacation may not be discouraged verbally, the inference exists within the culture itself. There are those leaders for whom holidays and vacations personally have no value and they assume everyone working under them should feel the same way, but everyone is not driven in that same way. I think we have all gone through seasons when longer hours and sacrifice were required. But a lifestyle dictated by long hours and sleep deprivation can have long-term negative consequences. Is there a true benefit to the long hours?

Research shows people are more productive long term when they have a good work/life balance. Why? Because they are typically happier, healthier, more balanced people. This research suggests that working long hours, more than 60 hours a week, gives only a small initial productivity boost. After three or four weeks, productively levels actually decline (Covert 2014).

Why should smart leaders promote a healthier work/life balance? The answer is quite simple, really. People need to disconnect from work, no matter how great the culture is. You may experience short-term gains from peddling the view that taking a vacation shows weakness or that an employee is not committed, but in the long run, employees managed under this philosophy will inevitably disengage at some point. Vacations give employees the opportunity to disconnect and disengage in a healthy, productive way. Without a planned time to disconnect, they will eventually disconnect permanently in a way that impacts their motivation and production levels.

According to a survey conducted by CareerBuilder, of people looking to change jobs, 39% are making the change because they are looking for a company with a better work/life balance. Did you get that? Basically 39% of the people who are leaving your company are doing so because the work/life balance in your culture sucks. (I'm sorry; was that harsh?) Of those employees who are *staying* in their current jobs, 50% are staying because they are happy with the work/life balance of their current company (Smith 2014).

Some leaders have the view that their employees are expendable; that there is an unlimited pool of people to fill jobs. These types of leaders tend to create cultures of fear and stress and employees are hesitant to take time off because of the fear of losing their position.

Americans have less available vacation time compared to other countries and tend to not use the time they do have. My wife and I worked for a company to which we were very committed. We took very little time off during our tenure there, until we had a disconnect over an expressed opinion. We owned a small percentage of the company but because one of the owners disliked our opinion on a matter—an opinion he solicited –our relationship was terminated. We were disappointed that our commitment to the company, which we'd evidenced by the little time off we had taken, didn't provide more currency in the situation. The time sacrifice we had made did not give us the currency we had thought.

Examples of a Healthy Work/Life Balance
Bandwidth is an IP-based communication technology company. They state that their mission (a reflection their company values) is to "unlock remarkable value for our customers." In an article written by Erica Anderson in *Forbes* magazine December 23, 2013, CEO David Morken was interviewed. I found his comments intriguing (because they prove my point). According to Morken, in order for Bandwidth to achieve the goal set out in their mission statement, the company must "'unlock remarkable value' for their employees: making Bandwidth a place that supports employees' body, mind and spirit."

Bandwidth has a strict rule that when an employee is on

vacation, no one from the company can communicate with them and the employee cannot communicate with anyone in the company. This rule is so strictly monitored, violations merit a call from the CEO reminding the employee that they're on vacation and should not be communicating with the office. In addition, taking vacation days is mandatory and the days must all be taken in the year in which they are received. They've tried to close up any loopholes for those who look for ways to circumvent the rules and simply not take vacation. (It's a sick world out there, I know!)

So how has this impacted the employees of Bandwidth? Employee vacations are actually rejuvenating, making for happier, healthier employees when they return to work. In addition, managers are more diligent in their efforts to develop their people because they know their people have to run the place while they are away during their own vacation. (Developing your people; now there's another novel idea.) Leaders are forced to give as much clarity as possible before leaving on vacation so employees know how to handle things in their absence. Morken believes this has a ripple effect (my words) and impacts the clarity of communication and increased levels of trust in the everyday interactions of managers and their people (all that from taking a vacation).

But it doesn't stop there. Bandwidth allows for a 90-minute lunch to give employees ample time to purse fitness. In case you were wondering, this is *paid time.* This is a voluntary program but that doesn't diminish its importance. The *Forbes* article states that according to Morken, since "everyone has limited time outside of work to be a significant other, a parent, a friend, or to pursue other non-work passions, making time for fitness during work hours makes it more likely that employees will both get and stay fit, and have time to focus on the non-work parts of their lives—improving both morale and productivity."

How is all this affecting Bandwidth's bottom line? After all, that is really what's most important in business, right? Bandwidth's results prove my contention that work/life balance benefits everyone: Bandwidth was set to make $150 million by close of 2013, up 20% from the previous year, and they were anticipating $200 million in profitable revenues in fiscal 2014 (Anderson 2013). So much for the myth that vacations are a cost without benefit to the employer.

Tony Schwartz is the president, founder, and CEO of The Energy Project and the best-selling author of *Be Excellent at Anything.* At his company, employees receive four weeks of vacation from their first year. In an op-ed piece he wrote for the *New York Times,* this is what he had to say about work/life balance: "Taking more time off is counterintuitive for most of us. The idea is also at odds with the prevailing work ethic in most companies, where downtime is typically viewed as time wasted. More than one-third of employees, for example, eat lunch at their desks on a regular basis. More than 50 percent assume they'll work during their vacations. In most workplaces, rewards still accrue to those who push the hardest and most continuously over time. But that doesn't mean they're the most productive" (Schwartz 2013).

In that same piece, Schwartz cites some additional facts drawn from other companies' experiences. This is what he reported: "In 2006, the accounting firm Ernst & Young did an internal study of its employees and found that for each additional 10 hours of vacation employees took, their year-end performance ratings from supervisors (on a scale of one to five) improved by 8 percent. Frequent vacationers were also significantly less likely to leave the firm" (Schwartz 2013).

In another piece written for the *New York Times,* Schwartz cites a 2012 Global Workforce Study conducted by the consulting firm Towers Watson. This study measured the relationship between employee engagement, meaning the willingness of employees to actually give their best effort at work, and financial results. The most highly engaged employees cited their ability to maintain their energy and enthusiasm at work as being the key to their success. In the article Schwartz states, "The differentiating factor among companies with the most highly engaged employees was an environment that supported people's physical, emotional and social well-being. Companies that did this least well had an average operating margin of 10 percent. Companies that best supported employees had an average operating margin of 27 percent" (Schwartz 2013). People like Tony Schwartz are very generous to their employees, giving them plenty of opportunities for vacation, because they believe—*they know*—that healthy employees are more productive not only in terms of output but also in terms of innovation and creativity.

Ryan Carson, CEO of Treehouse, started his company on a four-day workweek. Not a four-day, ten-hour workweek; a four-day, 32-hour workweek. The company has maintained a yearly growth rate of 120% and annual sales of ten million with a workforce of 70 employees. You must be thinking that they pay people at lower rates, right? Wrong. According to Carson, they still pay full salaries and offer a generous benefits package. As you might imagine, this gives them a definite recruiting edge, has led to high retention rates and has had a significant impact on morale. The consistent three-day weekend means come Monday, people are refreshed and excited to come back to work (that's been my personal experience when I have had a three-day weekend). Of course the real kicker is employees have 50% more time to spend with family, pursuing hobbies and outside interests. (You're probably wondering right about now how you can apply to work there.) Carson believes because of the compressed week, the quality of work is higher and there really are no slow, down days. His employees find the four-day workweek to be agreeable and have been known to respond to outside companies seeking to recruit them with the question, "Have you gone to a four-day workweek yet?"

Gaining popularity among companies is the implementation of a 9/80 work schedule. This schedule allows employees to work eight 9-hour days and have every other Friday off. The employees are divided into A and B schedules so everyone does not have to be off at the same time. As you might guess, this kind of schedule has a huge appeal and is embraced by the majority of employees. Even though it is not as edgy as Treehouse's 32-hour workweek, the warm reception the 9/80 schedule receives is another indicator that people embrace the idea of a flexible scheduling to allow for better work/life balance, both millennials and veteran employees.

Why the Poor Work/Life Balance

But not all companies are quick to embrace the idea. According to Jessica DeGroot, founder of the Third Path Institute, there are two primary reasons the four-day workweek is a hard sell. The first reason is the existence of strong organizational norms that have dictated for years who gets ahead at work (who acquires currency). DeGroot says managers tend to promote staffers who "put work first," which typically means showing up every weekday. Second, four-day workweeks add complexity to managers' jobs. Says DeGroot, "It's much easier to say to everyone, 'Come in at the same time every day and work long hours'" (Eisenberg 2013).

From the beginning, I have said work/life balance is about value. Working 60 hours a week seems to be more in keeping with the American work ethic. Working long hours has long been equated to a having a high commitment to your work. Some people experience a tremendous amount of guilt and anxiety if they don't work long hours and take time off. Unfortunately, those long hours without ever unplugging can directly conflict with the reason you go to work, like your commitment to your family, but they also impact your overall well-being. There are those annoying testimonials by successful millionaires who claim that a 60-hour work week is the path to success. If you believe what Tim Ferriss says in his book, *The 4-Hour Workweek,* working 60 hours is not required to become successful—that much of what we fill those hours with is inefficient and unproductive anyway.

Treehouse worked at eliminating all the inefficiencies in a normal workplace and found ways to make the 32-hour workweek just as effective as a 40-plus-hour week. And these changes were very sustainable. That's a definite myth buster! Have we bought into the mindset that in order to be successful and remain true to the American work ethic, we must work long hours? What about the inefficiencies that convolute those long hours? All too often, we adopt a value-based mindset that has no basis in what is really true. I don't know about you but if I am going to give my time, I want it to mean something, be an efficient use of resources and contribute to my work/life balance—not dilute it. In many instances, the long hours are simply a result of bad management practices, poor work processes, and misguided thinking about what truly makes a good employee.

A Personal Account

When our kids were older, my wife and I were able to take some time off, just the two of us. Raising six kids, we had been in it for a long haul. For our first trip we chose a cruise, an excellent choice, I might say. I found the trip to be a great time of self-renewal and healthy disconnect. I felt a little guilty leaving my kids behind but once on the trip, I realized it was the right decision. After this first cruise, on my first day back to work, one of my co-workers commented that I must have had a good time because I was glowing. Okay, there was that "alone with my wife no kids" thing, but I realized that the time away from work, too, had such a tremendous impact on my well-being that it affected my outward appearance. To be honest, we had forgotten what it was like to truly relax and recharge our batteries. Since that time, we have taken other trips and I now refuse to let the myths that surround the American business culture inhibit me from taking time off because I know the time off contributes to making me a more productive person and employee.

The American business culture is ripe for a new breed of smarter leaders to consider the impact of work/life balance on their people and how it impacts their ability to deliver at higher levels of productivity. Proper work/life balance is an integral part of a thriving work culture and plays a key role in maintaining employee engagement, eliminating both mental and physical disconnect. Don't underestimate its potential to heighten performance or, in its absence, lessen the overall efficiency of your company. I think that a large of part of "finding the laughter" will be over delivering in this area, generously providing time off for your people, not counting it as weakness or a lack of commitment when they take it. ∎

CHAPTER TWELVE

Recruiting and Retention
The Secret

"We've actually passed on a lot of smart, talented people that we know can make an immediate impact on our top or bottom line but if they're not good for our culture then we won't hire them for that reason alone."

—Tony Hsieh

Retention levels should be telling you the story of your culture. They are certainly telling you something about your leadership. If good people are leaving, it would be worth your time to find out why. Yet I see managers time and again give no consideration to retention levels. Eliminating those things we have talked about that create disconnect and promoting those dynamics that engage people will have a positive impact on your retention levels.

One Last Take on Mr. Welch
Perhaps the main reason I don't really believe in Jack Welch's

idea of the top 20% is because I think there is so much un-developed and undiscovered talent in the marketplace that assessments of those who are considered the top talent are characteristically inaccurate. At the risk of repeating myself, that idea creates a culture where those who are considered the top talent are well fed and the rest get the scraps, a system that is self-propagating and which we justify under the guise of healthy competition. This style of management can result in low retention levels because of the type of culture it creates for the remaining 80%.

Better Management Styles: A Few Examples

Whole Foods rejects the idea of ranking employees into the 20/70/10 profile. In their assessment, this creates a fear-based culture that damages morale and pits people against each other. In this culture, employees see themselves as rivals instead of teammates (Mackey 2014). Mackey, in his book *Conscious Capitalism,* contends that more is gained when people collaborate as a team, competing against other teams within the company to earn rewards and increase overall company achievement, not as a means to slot people for termination. Whole Foods is proving the value of this management philosophy with less than a 10% employee turnover rate on an annual basis. With the higher retention rates, Whole Foods can afford to invest more of their dollars into training and development, a win-win for both the company and employees.

Another company, Costco Wholesale, has had the lowest turnover rate in the retail business for over three decades; five times lower than their competitor Walmart. Costco is known for offering its employees comprehensive health coverage covering 90% of the costs and highly competitive salaries, paying employees an average of $17 an hour. The grumblers on Wall Street claim Costco cares more about its employees and customers than it does its shareholders, but former CEO James Sinegal, during his time at the helm of the company, saw these kinds of practices as an investment and the best of business practices. If the proof is in the pudding, then the 70% revenue growth over the past five years and doubling of its stock prices is telling the real story. We talked earlier in the book about the disproportionate measure of currency, both monetary and non-monetary. I think it is worth noting that James Sinegal opted to take a low annual salary of $350,000 (this is low as compared to other CEOs of similar size companies in his industry). That amount was not arbitrary. It was just 12 times the rate paid to the typical Costco employee.

The Impact of Perception on Retention Rates

Perhaps there is no other factor more responsible for poor hiring practices, whether it is recruiting someone new or handing out promotions, than that of perception. We talked about perception earlier. It is an unruly dictator in the workplace, in part because of its close association with bias. We can all acknowledge the fact that perception often dictates reality, whether it reflects what is actually true or not. We let it influence our judgments about people, even if they are inaccurate. Perception puts people in a box, one from which it is hard to break out. When that box determines the amount of workplace currency a person is allowed, that can be very frustrating. In those cases where a person is trapped within the perception box, it is very difficult for them to show who they really are.

People, out of necessity, have made themselves masters at projecting the right image to gain the currency needed to get hired or find their way up the promotional ladder. I understand the importance of image and how it plays in currency. But realize that character is driving some people and they don't like the deception that sometimes accompanies image. Look beyond the image and make sure you find the true character behind it. Those who fail to do this often end up hiring a person based on an appearance, possibly one that played into their own bias. In hindsight, maybe that person turned out to be a good choice and maybe they didn't. The scary thing is, we often don't really know until that person is on the job for a while, and if they are really masters of projecting the right image, their true self can go undiscovered until they finally get promoted to management. Now supervising other people, everyone is left scratching their heads, saying, "How in the world did that person get to this position?" By that time, nobody really knows.

I am always amazed at the talented, hardworking people who get passed over for promotion all because of the faulty, biased perceptions of decision makers. Such situations create a lot of disconnect in the workplace and ultimately lead to disengaged workers. What happens to these talented, hardworking people who are repeatedly passed over? They eventually head out the door—hopefully on their own initiative.

We all are a bit arrogant in that we typically like people who are just like us and as managers; we tend to hire people like ourselves. The problem is, these people typically have the same weaknesses and look at things the same way that we do. The secret of an extraordinary team is diversity, if there is strong collaboration and good communication within the group. Smart leaders look to build their teams with a diverse group of people who are not altogether alike. They don't all have to be star players; in fact, many times the star players can be a detriment to the development of the rest of the team.

Recognition

If you remember, recognition is part of what makes up currency in the workplace. Perception is the enemy of proper recognition. When perception-based decisions overtake proper recognition, we let talented people slip through our fingers. One of my favorite movie scenes is from *The Mask of Zorro*. Two Mexican brothers and a third white male partner are thieves working a con masquerading as two prisoners and a bounty hunter. The two Mexican brothers are pretending to be the prisoners. The white man is pretending to be the bounty hunter. They come upon the local Mexican police station with the brothers tied up behind the bounty hunter, who has the "Reward" poster in hand. He begins proclaiming that he has captured the famous "Murrieta" brothers, and he is there to collect the bounty. Once the police confirm they are the two thieves on the poster, they try to exert their authority and take the brothers into their custody without having to pay the bounty. This leads to a struggle and in the midst of it, one of the Mexican policemen hits the younger brother. The older brother, who still looks to be tied up as part of the masquerade, pulls a gun out of the back of his pants and points it at the police officer's face and says in his Mexican accent, "Touch my brother again and I will kill you." The police officer, very much taken by surprise, responds in his Mexican accent, "I thought you were tied up" to which the older brother responds, "That is because you are stupid."

Like the Mexican police officer, we are often fooled by appearances. If, as a leader, you are making decision based on an appearance, there is a good chance you are opening yourself up to be misled. You may regretfully discover later that you made a bad decision, saying to yourself in your best Mexican accent, "I thought he was a good choice." I will then say back to you in my best Mexican accent, "That's because you are stupid."

The secret to recruiting is proper recognition, free of misperception and bias. Unfortunately, the interview process can become very convoluted and many talented people often go undiscovered. Many companies are reassessing their hiring practices for this very reason.

Let's look at Google, who in the beginning hired people on the basis of who came from the best schools with the highest GPAs. From experience, they now recognize that the best talent is not always the people who have degrees and high GPAs. Currently, 14% of their teams are made up of people without degrees. They have put higher premiums on the soft skills—leadership, humility, collaboration, adaptability and a love for learning (Friedman 2014).

Laszlo Bock, the senior vice president of people operations for Google, determined GPAs and test scores are worthless as hiring criteria and a poor predictor of performance. According to Bock, the least valuable players are those who see themselves as the "experts." Instead, he looks for people with a high degree of cognitive ability, who are innately curious, eager to learn and have promising leadership skills (Friedman 2014). Smart leaders have trained themselves to look beyond appearance and the traditional ways of recruiting and promoting that have proven to be ineffective, recognizing the potential in a person is not always immediately obvious.

Beware of the Dominating Personalities

As a young couple, my wife and I would hang out with other young couples at different events. Every year, we went to a Valentine's Day party with the same group of friends. There was one couple in particular of which the husband was very much the life of the party type, outgoing and quick-witted. He was definitely the dominant personality in the room. I am not sure whether no one thought they could compete with his quick wit or maybe everyone was so used to him dominating the party, the rest of us just didn't bother trying to share the limelight with him. Then one year, this couple didn't show up. The first thing I noticed was the group dynamics changed drastically with his absence. All of a sudden, instead of one guy cracking jokes, now there were five or six guys filling the party with quick wit and humor; in fact, the whole room was more socially alive and it turned out to be one of the best Valentine's Day parties we attended. The only significant change was the absence of that one husband.

Now let's say I was a hiring manager looking for quick-witted people. At all the other parties, I would have only seen the one guy with the quick wit. Yet there were others in the room who were just as funny and just as quick-witted, but who were being overshadowed by the one dominant personality. The most interesting group dynamic is that those five or six who proved to be equally quick-witted and funny, now that the dominant person was removed from the mix, were much more collaborative as a group in that they didn't feel the need to overshadow the others. Their non-competitive attitudes that kept them from challenging the one individual now proved to be of value. The team dynamic was much improved and the party was much more enjoyable. If I was a recruiter at the last party, I would have found five or six people with the skills I was looking for, in contrast to just finding the one at the other parties.

Great individuals may found companies, but great companies are built by great teams. In business, I have seen leaders gravitate to one or two dominant individuals. Perhaps it is human nature to gravitate toward the dominant personality, but as smart leaders, we must resist this tendency and make sure we are cultivating the whole of our available talent. We typically think the burden is on the worker to showcase his or her talent on the job, and this is certainly true in part. But as leaders, we must provide the stage and props to allow opportunity for everyone to showcase their abilities, making sure we are not creating a performance box for someone based on their personality.

I rarely look at my top performers as a gauge of my leadership ability. I examine my average performer, looking for ways to challenge him to perform at a higher level, and gauge my leadership ability by the arc of his improvement. You would be surprised at the degree of loyalty such an attitude will inspire in those people.

Smart leaders take ordinary people and make them into extraordinary people. Leaders should begin with the basic premise that every person is capable of extraordinary accomplishment. This is just as easy as assuming they will disappoint you. Does that mean every person will aspire to that kind of achievement? No, but your success rate will be much higher if you start with the more optimistic premise.

Going Against the System

Moneyball, Michael Lewis' book which later was made into a motion picture starring Brad Pitt and Jonah Hill, is one of my favorite stories because it demonstrates how a leader went against traditional recruiting practices in a very old system and changed the face of baseball. The baseball mindset at the time was that big names, strong athletic hitters and young pitchers who threw fast pitches were the staples of a successful ball club. In other words, great teams were built on star players. Unfortunately for Billy Beane, the general manager of the Oakland A's, he didn't have the kind of budget to work with that would allow him to recruit this recognized top-shelf talent, so he was forced to find alternatives.

Enter the analytical, evidence-based and never before heard of sabermetric approach to hiring players. This approach flew directly in the face of the traditional ways clubs would recruit players. The sabermetric approach drew Beane's attention to undervalued players in the market. Sabermetrics showed these players to be hitters with high on-base percentages and pitchers who produced a lot of ground outs. According to sabermetrics, these are the types of players who win games. This approach took Beane to the playoffs in both 2002 and 2003. This new kind of winning team was made up of young, affordable players and less expensive veterans who had been written off by the baseball establishment.

Michael Lewis, in an interview with Billy Beane, sets forth Beane's management philosophy: "The minute you feel like you have to do something, you're screwed; you can always recover from the player you didn't sign, but you may never recover from the player that you did sign that you shouldn't have. And baseball is littered with teams that have signed punitive superstars to huge contracts who then don't pan out. And the franchises are wounded or sometimes severely crippled by the fact that they don't have any money left to go and pay other players, and they're left with this superstar who's not performing and earning $80 million. In baseball, it makes much less sense to do this than in most sports because one guy on a baseball team rarely makes that much difference. It really is a team sport. So the notion that you've got to sign this superstar or that superstar is really a little silly, and that's the first principle of Billy Beane's school of management" (Lewis 2003). With Beane's success, the ideas behind sabermetrics changed the way the industry had traditionally viewed recruiting. Someone dared to do it differently.

Sending the Wrong Message
My son played football for three years for a youth sports league. The very first year, the team had one star player whom the coaches depended on to carry them through the season. This worked the majority of the season until the playoffs, when they only made it to the second round. This was my son's first year to play and I remember the coach apologizing at the end of the season for not working with him more. The coach said my son had potential, but I was a little confused

as to why little effort was given to developing that potential. Nonetheless, we were just happy that he did get some playing time that season.

When the second year rolled around, the coach's star player was no longer with the team. It was the norm for the same players and coaches to move up together from year to year, so the team had the same players minus their star player from the previous year. There were a few strong defensive players, but the team performed miserably and had a losing season.

In the third season, a few of the stronger players were lost to other teams as they defected due to the previous losing season. There was a coaching change, but the season started the same way the last one ended. With continued loses, the new coach decided to ask his brother, a reputable coach elsewhere, to come observe the team.

I had my own suspicions as to why the team was not performing well. After observing the team, the visiting coach confirmed my suspicions. In his assessment, the team as a whole did not have a good grasp of the fundamentals.

Let's summarize the events. The first year, the coaches looked to the star player to take them to a winning season. This had carried them in the first year up to the playoffs, but no further. Because they had a decent winning season, there was no reason to evaluate the team's performance. The second year, the remaining players couldn't carry them to a successful season and they lost the remaining stronger talent. This prompted some evaluation, bringing about the coaching staff change. Finally, they brought in an outside party to evaluate. The answer turned out to be quite simple—the coaching staff had failed to train the whole of their players in the basic fundamentals of the game, only focusing on certain individuals whom they hoped would bring them a winning season. They sacrificed the team's success in their search for superstars. It sent the wrong message to the other players.

This story could have just as easily fit under the chapter on development, but I wanted to illustrate that building a winning team is not about recruiting superstars; it is about discovering and developing the potential in people. It is all tightly woven together: development, motivation, engagement, retention, success.

The Secret to Retention

The secret to retention is, there is no secret to retention. Those employees with higher workplace currency stay the longest. Where there is a culture with the opportunity to develop, where personal growth is encouraged, where people feel connected in a collaborative, trusting environment, where they are invested because they have a voice in the workplace, where the company encourages a healthy work/life balance, people will tend to stick around. This all translates into an exceptional and engaging culture. It is the currency of culture. It's not rocket science. It's just Smart Leadership. ▪

References

Schultz, Howard. 2012. *Onward: How Starbucks Fought for Its Life without Losing Its Soul* (Emmaus, PA: Rodale Books, 2012).

Guerrera, Francesco. 2009. "Welch condemns share price focus." *Financial Times,* March 12, 2009. http://www.ft.com/cms/s/0/294ff1f2-0f27-11de-ba10-0000779fd2ac.html#axzz3Gpy318ww.

Berger, Jonah. 2013. *Contagious: Why Things Catch On* (New York: Simon and Schuster, 2013).

Pink, Daniel H. 2011. *Drive: The Surprising Truth About What Motivates Us* (New York: Riverhead Books, 2011).

Welch, Jack. 2013. "Jack Welch: 'Rank-and-Yank'? That's Not How It's Done." *Wall Street Journal,* November 14, 2013.

The Naïve Optimist Blog; "No Managers: Why We Removed Bosses at Treehouse," blog entry by Ryan Carson, September 17, 2003.

Tuttle, Brad. 2013. "The 5 big mistakes that led to Ron Johnson's ouster at JC Penney." *Time.com,* April 9, 2013. http://business.time.com/2013/04/09/the-5-big-mistakes-that-led-to-ron-johnsons-ouster-at-jc-penney/.

Wray, Andrew. 2012. "Former Apple manager tells how the original iPhone was developed, why it went with Gorilla Glass." *iMore.com,* Saturday, February 4, 2012. http://www.imore.com/apple-manager-tells-original-iphone-born.

Valukas, Anton R. 2014. "Report to Board of Directors of General Motors Company Regarding Ignition Switch Recalls." May 29, 2014. Page 258.

Isidore, Chris. 2014. "Safety regulators at NHTSA share blame for GM recall failure." *Money.CNN.com,* September 16, 2014. http://money.cnn.com/2014/09/16/news/companies/gm-recall-nhtsa/.

Bennett, Jeff. 2014. "GM to Recall 8.45 Million More Vehicles in North America." *Wall Street Journal,* June 30, 2014.

Hirsch, Jerry and Jim Puzzanghera. 2014. "Lawmaker: GM response to ignition switch issue 'smacks of cover-up'." *Los Angeles Times Business/Auto,* June 18, 2014.

Tulgan, Bruce. 2014. "The Under-management Epidemic Report 2014:... Ten Years Later." http://rainmakerthinking.com/assets/uploads/2014/04/Undermanagement-Epidemic-WP1.pdf.

Southwest Corporate Fact Sheet. http://www.swamedia.com/channels/Corporate-Fact-Sheet/pages/corporate-fact-sheet.

Gittell, Jody. 2003. *The Southwest Airlines Way: Using the Power of Relationships to Achieve High Performance* (New York: McGraw-Hill, 2005).

Maxon, Terry. 2014. "Southwest Airlines says profit sharing will reach $228 million in 2014." *The Dallas Morning News,* April 14, 2014. http://aviationblog.dallasnews.com/2014/04/southwest-airlines-says-profit-sharing-will-reach-228-million-in-2014.html/.

Mackey, John and Raj Sisodia. 2014. *Conscious Capitalism* (Cambridge: Harvard Business School Publishing Corporation, 2014) page 18, 34, 35, 46, 47, 50, 87, 90, 91, 92.

Stone, Brad and Adam Satariano. 2014. "Tim Cook Interview: The iPhone 6, the Apple Watch, and Remaking a Company's Culture." *Businessweek.com,* September 18, 2014. http://www.businessweek.com/articles/2014-09-17/tim-cook-interview-the-iphone-6-the-apple-watch-and-being-nice.

References

Pepitone, Julianne. 2013. "Microsoft kills employee-ranking system." *CNNMoney.com*, November 13, 2013. http://money. cnn.com/2013/11/13/technology/enterprise/microsoft-stack-ranking/.

Eichenwald, Kurt. 2012. "Microsoft's Lost Decade." *Vanity Fair*, August 2012. http://www.vanityfair.com/business/2012/08/microsoft-lost-mojo-steve-ballmer.

Wingfield, Nick. 2013. "Microsoft Abolishes Employee Evaluation System." *New York Times*, November 13, 2013. http://bits.blogs.nytimes.com/2013/11/13/microsoft-abolishes-employee-evaluation-system/?_php=true&_type=blogs&_r=0.

Reck, Ross. "Case Study: Google." *RossReck.com*. http://rossreck. com/media/i/Google_CaseStudy.pdf.

Marmot, Sir Michael. 2002. Interview by Harry Kriesler, *Conversations with History, Institute of International Studies*, UC Berkeley, March 18, 2002, http://globetrotter.berkeley.edu/people2/Marmot/marmot-con3.html.

Gladwell, Malcolm. 2008. *Outliers* (New York: Back Bay Books/ Little, Brown and Company, 2008) page 22, 24, 25.

Goleman, Daniel, Richard Boyatzis and Annie McKee. 2013. *Primal Leadership: Realizing the Power of Emotional Intelligence* (Boston: Harvard Business Review Press, 2013).

Schultz, Howard. 1997. *Pour Your Heart Into It: How Starbucks Built a Company One Cup at a Time* (New York: Hyperion, 1997).

Goffee, Rob and Gareth Jones. 2013. "Creating the Best Work-place on Earth," *Harvard Business Review*, May 2013, http:// hbr.org/2013/05/creating-the-best-workplace-on-earth/ar/1.

Summer, Nick. 2014. "The Trouble with IBM," *Bloomberg Business Week*, Technology, May 22, 2014.

Webley, Kayla. 2010. "100 Days of the BP Spill: A Timeline," *Time,* http://content.time.com/time/interactive/ 0,31813,2006455,00.html.

Walsh, Brian. 2010. "Oil Spill: Goodbye, Mr. Hayward," *Time,* http://science.time.com/2010/07/25/oil-spill-goodbye-mr-hayward/.

Walt, Vivienne. 2010. "Can BP Ever Rebuild Its Reputation," *Time,* July 19, 2010, http://content.time.com/time/business/ article/0,8599,2004701,00.html.

Bethune, Gordon. 1998. *From Worst to First: Behind the Scenes of Continental's Remarkable Comeback* (New York: John Wiley & Sons, Inc., 1998).

Covert, Bryce. 2014. "This Company Has A 4-Day Work Week, Pays Its Workers A Full Salary And Is Super Successful," *ThinkProgress.org,* April 18, 2014, http://thinkprogress.org/ economy/2014/04/18/3428463/treehouse-four-day-workweek/.

Smith, Jacquelyn. 2014. "Why Your Top Talent Is Leaving In 2014, And What It'll Take To Retain Them," *Forbes,* January 24, 2014, http://www.forbes.com/sites/ jacquelynsmith/2014/01/24/why-your-top-talent-is-leaving-in-2014-and-what-itll-take-to-retain-them/.

Anderson, Erika. 2013. "Want To Succeed? Don't Check Your Email – And Work Out At Lunch," *Forbes,* December 23, 2013, http://www.forbes.com/sites/erikaandersen/2013/12/23/want-to-succeed-dont-check-your-email-and-work-out-at-lunch/.

Schwartz, Tony. 2011. *Be Excellent at Anything* (New York: Free Press, 2011).

Schwartz, Tony. 2013. "Relax! You'll Be More Productive," *The New York Times,* February 9, 2013, http://www.nytimes.com/2013/02/10/opinion/sunday/relax-youll-be-more-productive.html?pagewanted=all.

References

Schwartz, Tony. 2013. "The Overlooked Secret to Great Performance," *The New York Times,* November 27, 2013, http://dealbook.nytimes.com/2013/11/27/the-overlooked-secret-to-great-performance/.

Eisenberg, Richard. 2013. "It's High Time For The 4-Day Workweek," *Forbes,* August 30, 2013, http://www.forbes.com/sites/nextavenue/2013/08/30/its-high-time-for-the-4-day-workweek/.

Keller, Gary and Jay Papasan. 2012. *The One Thing* (New York: Relleck Publishing Partners, Ltd, 2012) page 98-99.

Friedman, Thomas L. 2014. "How to Get a Job at Google," *The New York Times,* February 22, 2014.

Billy Beane, interview by Michael Lewis, National Public Radio *npr.org,* May 28, 2003, http://www.npr.org/2011/09/23/140703403/moneyball-tracking-down-how-stats-win-games.

Merriam-Webster Online Dictionary and Thesaurus, Merriam-Webster Publishing Company, 2014, http://www.merriam-webster.com/top-ten-lists/2014-word-of-the-year/culture.html.

Author. Speaker.
Thought Leader.
Brett M. Hutton

Brett M. Hutton is an American leadership author, thought leader, speaker, husband and father of six. He has spent over 30 years working in and studying American business in the banking, customer service, retail, internet sales, and oil and gas industries. His research of America's leading culture driven businesses has included in depth studies of Whole Foods, Starbucks, Costco, Zappos, and other leading businesses.

His innovative and creative approach to leadership has been proven to be effective in multiple industries and workplaces. Speaking to groups both large and small, he challenges his listeners to courageously rethink the antiquated approach to leadership corporate America has promoted for so long. He challenges audiences and readers to instead unlock the uniqueness that lies within each individual within an organization.

What Audiences Are Saying About Brett M. Hutton

"Brett's leadership style is very communicative. People can learn a more realistic approach to leadership through Brett; his ability to show appreciation toward the efforts of his team, to have open table discussions, and to have open lines of communication. I would recommend using Brett for any leadership speaking based off of my experience with him at our company and the impact he has had on our team."

Amber Burke, Manager at IPS Engineering

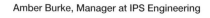

To Book Brett M. Hutton,
Please Contact:

Call: (918) 978-2838
E-mail: brett@brettmhutton.com
or Visit: www.brettmhutton.com